Voice and Mirroring in L2 Pronunciation Instruction

Applied Phonology and Pronunciation Teaching

*Series Editor – **Martha C. Pennington**, Birkbeck University of London*

The Applied Phonology and Pronunciation Teaching series seeks to provide a forum for dissemination of knowledge in the area of applied phonology and pronunciation teaching.

The series aims to provide information and stimulate conversations that can advance knowledge, understanding, and good practice in any of the areas of applied phonology and pronunciation teaching.

Voice and Mirroring in L2 Pronunciation Instruction

Darren LaScotte
Colleen Meyers
Elaine Tarone

SHEFFIELD UK   BRISTOL CT

Published by Equinox Publishing Ltd.

UK: Office 415, The Workstation, 15 Paternoster Row, Sheffield,
        South Yorkshire S1 2BX
USA: ISD, 70 Enterprise Drive, Bristol, CT 06010

www.equinoxpub.com

First published 2023

British Library Cataloguing-in-Publication Data
A catalogue record for this book is available from the British Library.

ISBN-13   978 1 80050 277 2   (hardback)
           978 1 80050 278 9   (paperback)
           978 1 80050 279 6   (ePDF)
           978 1 80050 315 1   (ePub)

Library of Congress Cataloging-in-Publication Data
Names: LaScotte, Darren K., author. | Meyers, Colleen M., 1951- author. | Tarone, Elaine, 1945- author.
Title: Voice and mirroring in L2 pronunciation instruction / Darren LaScotte, Colleen Meyers and Elaine Tarone.
Description: Sheffield, South Yorkshire ; Bristol, CT : Equinox Publishing Ltd., [2023] | Series: Applied phonology and pronunciation teaching | Includes bibliographical references and index. | Summary: "Voice and Mirroring in L2 Pronunciation Instruction presents an approach to teaching pronunciation which aims for learners to internalize the "voices" (complexes of linguistic and non-linguistic features that embody particular speakers' emotion, social stance, and group identification) of proficient speakers of the second language (L2). The audience for the volume includes language teachers, particularly those desiring to use top-down pedagogical approaches like the Mirroring Project to improve learners' intelligibility, and academic researchers interested in studying the way adults can acquire second language phonology by holistically adopting and channeling the voices of speakers they admire. The book is also of potential interest to language teacher educators, curriculum developers, and textbook writers"-- Provided by publisher.
Identifiers: LCCN 2022026056 (print) | LCCN 2022026057 (ebook) | ISBN 9781800502772 (hardback) | ISBN 9781800502789 (paperback) | ISBN 9781800502796 (ePDF) | ISBN 9781800503151 (ePub)
Subjects: LCSH: Language and languages--Study and teaching. | Language and languages--Pronunciation. | Grammar, Comparative and general--Phonology--Study and teaching. | Second language acquisition. | Fluency (Language learning)
Classification: LCC P53 .L3736 2023 (print) | LCC P53 (ebook) | DDC 418.0071--dc23/eng/20230113
LC record available at https://lccn.loc.gov/2022026056
LC ebook record available at https://lccn.loc.gov/2022026057

Typeset by S.J.I. Services, New Delhi, India

Contents

Series Editor's Preface

Voice and Mirroring in L2 Pronunciation Instruction offers a fresh perspective on pronunciation as a foundation for a novel teaching approach which the authors, a team that was first brought together by Elaine Tarone at the University of Minnesota, have researched and refined in collaboration with other colleagues over many years in the classroom. Starting from a broad, "top-down" orientation to language learning, LaScotte, Meyers, and Tarone describe pronunciation in psychological and sociocultural terms as a projection of a speaker's identity that is linked to the wider context of nonverbal behavior. This conceptualization of the nature of language learning and pronunciation is supported by a review of sociolinguistic research and is contrasted with the "bottom-up" perspective that has predominated in pronunciation research and teaching.

On this foundation, the authors build a case for teaching pronunciation as an activity of developing new personae, or "voices," in a second language. Their approach to creating an L2 voice aims for language learners to internalize the speech and nonverbal characteristics of a speaker whom individual learners select to be an aspirational model for their own communicative behavior. They study their model speaker's communicative performance, with a focus on suprasegmental features and nonverbal behaviors, and then go through a series of activities designed to lead to their being able to "mirror" their model's pronunciation, facial expressions, and body dynamics as exhibited in a videotaped speech sample. Building on these mirroring activities, the ultimate goal is for the learner to "channel," or transfer, the model speaker's persona in their own communicative performance.

The book is both practical and well-grounded in theory and research, and it should find a ready and appreciative audience among teachers and prospective teachers of pronunciation as well as researchers focusing on this aspect of language learning. The teaching approach, design, and procedures of the mirroring technique are presented in detail, with visual illustration and extensive discussion of before and after communicative profiles of learners who have applied mirroring to their own L2 performance, along with step-by-step instructions and worksheets ready for use with students. The result is an innovative best-practices volume on the teaching of pronunciation – one that provides an in-depth guide to an original teaching method backed up by research and a carefully constructed conceptual and theoretical base.

—Martha C. Pennington
Series Editor
Applied Phonology and Pronunciation Teaching

Acknowledgements

We would like to thank our families, colleagues, and the series editor Martha C. Pennington for their guidance and support. Grateful acknowledgment is also made to the following authors and publishers for permission to reprint previously published figures:

- Waveland Press for FIGURE 3.1. Illustration of Key Choice in Intonation Paragraphs, page 35.
- Cambridge University Press for FIGURE 4.1. An Elaborated Level III Psycholinguistic Model, page 47.
- Leah Moreno for FIGURE 4.2. Praat Display, "Matt" Voice v. "self" Voice, page 62.

List of Abbreviations

C2	The Culture that uses the L2
CAF	Complexity, Accuracy, and Fluency
CAT	Communication Accommodation Theory
CV	Consonant-Vowel
CVC	Consonant-Vowel-Consonant
ESL	English as a Second Language
IL	Interlanguage
IPA	International Phonetic Alphabet
ITA	International Teaching Assistant
L1	First Language
L2	Second or Foreign Language (any language learned after the L1)
LAD	Language Acquisition Device
MP	Mirroring Project
NL	Native Language
NNS	Non-Native Speaker
NS	Native Speaker
SAT	Speech Accommodation Theory
SCT	Sociocultural Theory
SLA	Second-Language Acquisition
TL	Target Language
UG	Universal Grammar

Chapter 1

Introduction to Voice and Mirroring in L2 Pronunciation Instruction

The Gileadites captured the fords of the Jordan leading to Ephraim, and whenever a survivor of Ephraim said, "Let me cross over," the men of Gilead asked him, "Are you an Ephraimite?" If he replied, "No," they said, "All right, say 'Shibboleth.'" If he said, "Sibboleth," because he could not pronounce the word correctly, they seized him and killed him at the fords of the Jordan. Forty-two thousand Ephraimites were killed at that time.

(New International Version Bible, 1978, Judges. 12:5–6)

In October 1937, the president of the Dominican Republic, Rafael Trujillo, devised a simple way to identify the Haitian immigrants living along the border of his country. Dominican soldiers would hold up a sprig of parsley – PEREJIL in Spanish – and ask people to identify it. Those who spoke Spanish would pronounce the word's central "r" with that language's characteristic trill; the Haitians, on the other hand, would bury the "r" sound in the throaty way of the French. To be on the receiving end of the parsley test would be to seal, either way, one's fate: The Spanish-speaking Dominicans were left to live, and the Haitians were slaughtered. It was a state-sponsored genocide that would be remembered, in one of history's greatest understatements, as the Parsley Massacre.

(Garber, 2015, para. 1)

*****

The quotations above make it abundantly clear in the most graphic of ways that pronunciation is not a trivial or surface-level aspect of second-language acquisition (SLA) and bilingualism. Indeed, a small difference in the way a speaker pronounces the one language they know can be tied so irrevocably to their fundamental identity, group membership, and loyalty that even when a speaker's life depends on it, that pronunciation cannot be modified. Teaching a learner in a classroom to pronounce an additional language with *nativeness* as a goal is not just a matter of asking them to mechanically repeat and form a new habit or change a physical behavior; it is literally asking them to be someone else – to change their very identities and emotional loyalties.

In this book, we offer an alternative top-down approach to learning and teaching the pronunciation of a second, or "foreign," language (hereafter, L2[1]). In consideration of research published since the 1970's showing the powerful impact of sociolinguistic context on L2 pronunciation, as well as recent SLA theoretical frameworks emphasizing the role of social and contextual factors in shaping interlanguage (IL) systems (e.g., Douglas Fir Group, 2016), we argue that a top-down orientation that begins with social context is preferred in both the research and the teaching of L2 pronunciation, and we offer our own original research on one top-down pedagogical activity – *mirroring* – which is rooted in socio-cultural perspectives on learning. We present an argument for a focus on pronunciation teaching that takes a speaker's identities, stances, and emotional expressions into account from the beginning, accepts them, and pursues the more pragmatic and achievable goals of *intelligibility* and *heteroglossia* rather than *nativeness* or the mastery of mechanical sounds and segments with a focus on sounding like an ideal native speaker of the target language.

Outline of the Book

In initial chapters of this book, we provide a chronological account of previously published and new unpublished findings in IL phonology which initially was dominated by a bottom-up orientation focused primarily on the decontextualized study of phonological segments and suprasegmentals, and which prioritized native-speaker accent as the learning goal. Over a period of decades, however, bottom-up research and teaching began to be supplemented by a top-down orientation that took social and physical context into account and established two new goals for pronunciation learning: understandability and representation of speaker identity.

In the first half of this book (Chapters 2 through 4), we review research that supports each of these goals, ending with variationist sociolinguistic and sociocultural models of SLA. Research studies on the latter demonstrate the way L2 learners can internalize the *voices* – complexes of linguistic and non-linguistic features that embody particular speakers' emotion, personal stance, and group identification – of proficient speakers of the L2, often dramatically (and unconsciously) shifting their pronunciation patterns as they enact these voices for their own purposes in both planned and unplanned speech. Such studies support the view that the construct of voice and the influence of social contextual factors in SLA are critical in shaping IL systems and raise a number of important implications for addressing learning outcomes in L2 pronunciation and understandability.

In the second half of this book (Chapters 5 through 6), we describe in detail top-down methods for teaching pronunciation, including those engaging language play, role-play, and drama techniques. We end with two case studies describing one of those methods, called the Mirroring Project, as an effective top-down pedagogy for teaching pronunciation and include instructional activities that have been used in a variety of teaching and learning settings in the United States (e.g., in International Teaching Assistant pronunciation course programs, intensive English language programs, and Adult Basic Education programs). We document the way this approach can help L2 learners modify their L2 pronunciation patterns and improve their understandability as they internalize and channel the voices of speakers they have selected as models.

In Appendix A, for teachers of L2 pronunciation who are interested in using the Mirroring Project with their own students, we share student worksheets we have developed in using it; notes for instructors are also provided in Appendix B.

Some Terminology

This book involves research and teaching focused on *pronunciation*, which is the act of producing the sounds of speech. The discipline of linguistics refers to the sounds of speech as *phonology*. The phonology of any language is made up of a unique set of sounds of speech organized into *segments* called *phonemes* (such as consonants and vowels), and *suprasegmentals*, or *prosody*, such as patterns of pitch (e.g., intonation and tone), and patterns of stress called *rhythm*. We learn the phonology of our native language (NL) or first language (L1) when we are very young and then effortlessly and unconsciously produce the speech sounds of our NL. However, when as adults we begin to learn an additional language, or L2, the process of learning its phonology is often a struggle.

Throughout this book, we use the term *IL phonology* in discussing both the research and teaching of the pronunciation of an L2. In doing this, we follow Selinker (1972) in defining IL as the autonomous linguistic system (including syntax, semantics, pragmatics, and phonology) which underlies learners' speech when they attempt to express meaning in the L2; it is distinct from but influenced by both the learner's NL and the target language (TL) being learned. The most fundamental claim of Selinker's interlanguage hypothesis is that the language produced by the adult learner when they attempt meaningful communication in a language being learned is systematic at every level: phonology, morphology, syntax, semantics, and pragmatics. As Selinker conceptualizes it, the linguistic system of IL, including its phonology, is the proper object of research on SLA, and an understanding of the way IL phonology develops in the mind of the learner is important in developing effective pedagogical interventions. IL phonology is a linguistic system being formed in the mind of the L2 learner. As such, IL phonology may be influenced not just by NL transfer and TL input, but also, to at least some extent, by language universals, developmental sequences, and pedagogy (transfer of training).

To begin our exploration, we provide a brief overview of the study and teaching of L2 pronunciation, which can assume either a *bottom-up* or a *top-down* orientation. According to Dalton and Seidlhofer (2000), a bottom-up approach tends to be structuralist, explicitly focusing on the acquisition and teaching of forms like phonemes in isolation, with little attention to their use in communication or to social context in general; the presumed goal of learning is a native-like accent. On the other hand, a top-down pedagogy is more communicative, and tends to prioritize social context, exploring the impact of factors like interlocutor roles and learner identity (and often, non-verbals) on segmental and prosodic features of phonology; here, the presumed goals of learning are understandability and an accent consistent with speaker identity.

A primary goal of a top-down pedagogy for L2 pronunciation learning is the ability to pronounce the L2 so that interlocutors can understand the speaker, despite their foreign accent. Levis (2005) provides a useful comparison of these bottom-up vs. top-down competing and essentially contradictory goals of native accent vs. understandability in pronunciation instruction, calling the first the *Nativeness Principle*, where the instructional objective is native-like pronunciation, and the second the *Intelligibility Principle*, where understandable pronunciation is the primary objective. According to Levis, the Nativeness Principle maintains that it is both possible and desirable for an adult learner to achieve a native-like accent in an L2, even though research has shown that this almost never occurs and that it appears to be biologically impossible. However, the

Intelligibility Principle offers such learners the alternative and achievable goal of being understandable, or comprehensible, to interlocutors, despite their foreign accent. For this purpose, Levis (2005) argues that instruction can in principle then focus on only those aspects of pronunciation that improve intelligibility; he points to Avery and Ehrlich's (1992) earlier claim that an instructional focus on prosody is more helpful than a focus on segmentals for communication with native speakers of the TL[2]. In this, Levis argues that this new learning goal must include an awareness of communicative context since intelligibility assumes both a speaker and a listener in interaction. He also mentions, but does not delve into, the importance of pronunciation and accent for speaker identity "as an essential marker of social belonging" (Levis, 2005, p. 375).

A central construct in this book involves the ability to make oneself understood by others. But what terms should we use to refer to a pronunciation goal of being understandable to TL speakers, and how should this construct be measured? For the purpose of focused research on SLA, Derwing and Munro (2015) propose the use of two related constructs of understandability: *intelligibility*, which is operationalized and measured as whether "listeners can understand the speaker's intended message" (p. 1) and *comprehensibility*, which is operationalized and measured as the degree of effort that interlocutors must exert in order to understand. Foote (2015, p. xii) provides very useful definitions of these two terms, which we reproduce exactly below, as we shall adopt them in this book:

Comprehensibility

The term refers to how difficult listeners find [L2] speech to understand; if they struggle and must listen carefully to understand an utterance, then this utterance would be considered as being low in comprehensibility, even if ultimately the message is understood (e.g., Derwing, Munro, & Thomson, 2008). In research, comprehensibility is usually measured using rating scales (e.g., Isaacs & Trofimovich, 2012; Munro & Derwing, 1995).

Intelligibility

Intelligibility refers to actual difficulty in understanding an utterance. Rather than using ratings, intelligibility is usually measured more objectively. For example, to derive a measure of intelligibility, listeners may be asked to transcribe an utterance rather than rate it (e.g., Munro, Derwing, & Morton, 2006). However, it should be noted that while this specific definition of intelligibility has become well accepted in [SLA] literature, it is also used more broadly to mean speech that is understandable, even by researchers in this field.

In this book, when we cite the research of others in the field, we will faithfully report the terms they use and the meanings they intend, whether intelligibility or comprehensibility. But when we are presenting our own research and pedagogical practices, we will use the term *intelligibility* in its general sense to mean understandability, or the ability to successfully negotiate meaning with an interlocutor by means of their spoken pronunciation and/or use of non-verbals, including gesture. Clearly, as Levis (2018) puts it, "nonnative speakers can be highly intelligible even when their speech is strongly accented" (p. 12). This point has been well established by research studies such as Munro and Derwing (2001) and Murphy (2014), which provide careful empirical evidence showing that even heavily accented speech can sometimes be perfectly intelligible to native speakers. In life, we know that U.S. television and film provide many examples of people whose spoken English accents are not like our own but who are nevertheless easy for us to understand. And obviously, the opposite can also be true: some people can be very hard for us to understand even if their accent is the same as our own. It seems obvious that the degree to which L2 learners are understandable must be studied and taught in social context in that it relies heavily on interactions with and perceptions of particular interlocutors with whom the L2 speaker interacts in communicative situations (Zielinski, 2008). Judgments of intelligibility involve contextual factors, where both the listener and the speaker are essential. As Levis (2005) reminds us, "[t]he intelligibility principle carries a sensitivity to context. Intelligibility assumes both a listener and a speaker..." (p. 372).

Chapter 1 in Review

In this chapter, we began with two quotations that illustrate in graphic detail how irrevocably linked pronunciation is to a speaker's fundamental identity, group membership, and loyalty – so much so that even when a speaker's life depends on it, that pronunciation cannot be modified. In consideration of this intimate connection of pronunciation to a speaker's individual and sociocultural profile, we suggested that a top-down pedagogy for teaching pronunciation is to be preferred over the bottom-up one often taken in teaching L2s such as English as a second language. After an outline of the contents of the book, we offered definitions of key terminology to be used in the book, including *pronunciation, phonology, segments, suprasegmentals, prosody,* and *rhythm.* We discussed in more depth the construct of *IL*, including *IL phonology*, which is the focus of this work, and we offered brief definitions of the constructs of *bottom-up* and *top-down* orientations to the research and teaching of IL phonology. Finally, we provided basic background on a core construct of the top-down approach that has been referred to in the literature using any of three related terms: *understandability*, *intelligibility*, and *comprehensibility*.

Chapter 1 Notes

1. By L2, we mean any language acquired by an individual after their first, or native language, has been acquired. Thus, L2 may refer to any subsequent language acquired, not just the second one.
2. Other research on English as an international language or lingua franca has argued for a principal focus on segmental instruction as opposed to suprasegmental instruction. While our book may be useful to all L2 pronunciation teachers and researchers, the research presented here may not apply to English as a lingua franca teaching and research contexts, and we encourage readers to review other available literature to fit their needs (cf. Jenkins, 2000).

Chapter 2

Bottom-Up and Top-Down Theories of Second-Language Acquisition

Orientation to Language and Learning

The bottom-up orientation is characterized by its structuralist means of describing language to learners, and also by the cognitivist learning theory that underlies it. Bottom-up research is decontextualized; neither social context nor communication in interaction is taken into account. In this chapter, we will review bottom-up research on IL phonology and pronunciation that predominated in the second half of the 20th century, as well as a small but growing amount of top-down scholarship and research initiated towards the close of the century.

Structuralist Language Analysis

A bottom-up orientation to the description of an L2 learner's phonology can be viewed as structuralist in the way it analyzes speech, in that the learner's stream of speech is described solely in terms of its physical and linguistic forms, without reference to the context of speaking. It is described primarily as a series of discrete linguistic segments (phonemes) with rules for vowel reduction and consonant blending in connected speech, but also – though to a lesser degree – as a set of accompanying rule-governed prosodic features consisting of intonation, stress, and rhythm. In this perspective, the goal or target of L2 learning is the accurate emulation of the pronunciation, or accent, of an imagined and idealized native speaker (NS) of the L2 (or rather, an idealized variety of the L2, the so-called "standard"). It is assumed that the L2 learner's goal is to be able to speak with the standard accent used by idealized NSs of the TL. For this reason, linguists go beyond just analyzing the learner's phonology as an independent system; they also compare it to the TL and NL systems, asking whether any particular IL phoneme or rule is correct or incorrect from the perspective of the standard TL accent. If the learner's accent is incorrect, containing errors, they typically assume that the cause is NL transfer – meaning, the learner is substituting a NL phoneme, prosodic pattern, or rule. For excellent and thorough examples of the structuralist method of describing and reshaping the L2 learner's phonology and comparing it to the standard TL accent in pedagogy, see Lado and Fries (1958) and Prator and Robinett (1985).

Although this bottom-up orientation to the study of IL, and especially IL phonology, dominated the field from the beginning, some researchers raised questions about it. L. Dickerson's (1975) study exposed some limits of this generally decontextualized and transfer-oriented approach when she showed that the learner's IL phonological system was one in which both positive and negative transfer operated variably. Depending on context, certain phonological contexts and tasks systematically encouraged more native-like (i.e., "correct") phonemes and accents than others. Building on the IL hypothesis, though still using this same structuralist and decontextualized research stance that focused on learners' errors in producing L2 phonemes, researchers such as Dickerson began to move beyond NL transfer as the sole cause of learner error or non-native accent.

Cognitivist Learning Theory

In terms of language learning, the bottom-up orientation is cognitivist or mentalist, and "conceives of the foreign language speaker as a deficient communicator struggling to overcome an underdeveloped L2 competence, striving to reach the 'target' competence of an idealized native speaker" (Firth & Wagner, 1997, p. 285). In so doing, this orientation gives little to no consideration to the way real-world speakers of the TL use a broad range of standard and non-standard varieties of the TL – including the use of different accents – to interact in real-world communities and contexts. Indeed, it is striking that few researchers in the late 20th and early 21st century – whatever their SLA cognitivist orientation, whether behaviorist, innatist, or developmental – went beyond structural descriptions of IL phonology to consider the influence of interaction, social context, or community norms in shaping and using that phonology. For SLA researchers assuming a structuralist and cognitivist perspective, L2 learners' IL phonology was treated as an abstract linguistic system that was completely divorced from pragmatics and social context, a system to be compared and contrasted with a standard accent that was assumed to be the learner's goal: the TL phonological system as used by ideal NSs. A considerable amount of research was carried out during the latter half of the 20th century using this predominantly structuralist and cognitivist methodology, far more than can be exhaustively reviewed here (see Johansson, 1973, and Major, 2001, for useful reviews).

Cognitivist Theories of SLA: Behaviorist, Innatist, and Developmental

Bottom-up theories of SLA focus on the way the human brain functions in acquiring and using language. These theories have provided different possible models for the way people learn to pronounce L2s.

Behaviorist learning theory focuses on the cognitive process of habit formation and learning by conditioning, whereby correct language production is praised and encouraged whereas incorrect language production receives negative feedback, possibly in the form of a correction (Skinner, 1957). This theory argues that since L2 learners by definition have already acquired an L1, the habits formed early and internalized in that NL may interfere with the formation of new habits in the TL and, if so, these erroneous habits must be corrected. Negative language transfer occurs when learners use such "old habits" in trying to produce the TL, and this was considered to be especially salient in IL phonology. To use a segmental example, the Spanish-speaking learner's habit of producing a consonant /r/ as a trill when communicating in English, as in Spanish, interferes with the formation of the new habit of producing an English consonant /ɹ/, which is an approximant (or, more specifically, a liquid). Much effort was devoted to the contrastive analysis of phonemes and phonological patterns of learners' NL in relation to those of the TL, so as to predict learners' errors both in pronunciation and perception of L2 speech. Such errors were argued at first to be exclusively caused by negative transfer: using sound patterns of the NL in place of the sound patterns of the TL. As described in Tarone (1978, pp. 16–18), such research often studied whether NL transfer affected learners' L2 pronunciation in experimental situations where learners were presented with TL words and sounds in isolation and asked to either produce them or perceive them. Good examples of such studies of L2 learners' perception of TL phonemes include Sapon and Carroll (1958), Scholes (1968), Singh and Black (1966), and K. Stevens, Libermann, Studdert-Kennedy, and Öhman (1969); and good examples of L2 learners' pronunciation of phonemes in their ILs include Brière (1966), Flege, Bohn, and Jang (1997), Johansson (1973), Nemser (1971), and Sheldon and Strange (1982).

Not long after Skinner (1957) published his theory on verbal behavior and learning by conditioning, Chomsky (1959) rebutted with a generative theory of linguistics which argued that all languages share the same properties and that the human brain has an innate ability to develop language systematically from infancy. In contrast to a behaviorist perspective which saw language learning as habit formation, Chomsky (1957, 1959) argued that behaviorism and habit-formation are incapable of explaining someone's ability to create new utterances they have never heard before. Rather, he proposed that language learning is accomplished by an innate part of the human mind – a language acquisition device (LAD) – which develops all human languages into creative tools that share common properties and have similar stages of development (i.e., Universal Grammar). This innatist perspective focused almost exclusively on cognition, and the autonomous mind soon became imagined as analogous to an information processor or computer. The so-called Universal Grammar (UG) theory of SLA focuses primarily on idealized (or decontextualized) linguistic structures, and not so much on pragmatics, or the social uses of linguistic structures in interactions to communicate intended meaning. Indeed, during the so-called "SLA Wars" of the 1990s, UG SLA researchers (e.g., Gregg, 1990, 1993), following Chomsky, explicitly dismissed learner language produced in social context as "performance" – something that played no part in the formation of the L2 learner's homogeneous (unvarying) "competence" or linguistic knowledge. Some researchers argue that processes of UG may occur in tandem with NL transfer to affect SLA. For example, Eckman's (1977, 1991) Markedness Differential Hypothesis suggested a possibly collaborative role for markedness as a form of linguistic universal. In this hypothesis, NL transfer could interact with markedness in universal implicational hierarchies such that unmarked phonological features of a TL would tend to be acquired before marked ones, regardless of whether those unmarked features occurred in the learner's NL.

As an example of such ease or difficulty of learning targets, in studying the syllable structure of IL phonology, Tarone (1980) identified a tendency among adult L2 learners, no matter what their NL, to produce open consonant-vowel (CV) patterned syllables to modify TL phonological sequences – even sequences that were the same as NL phonemic sequences. So for example, a Korean learner might substitute the CV syllable /ho:/ for English consonant-vowel-consonant (CVC) /ho:l/, deleting the final /l/, even though there is a Korean syllable /ko:l/. A Cantonese speaker might add a schwa vowel /ə/ to an unreleased /t/ stop consonant at the end of the English word *blanket* even though Cantonese has a CVC syllable /kat/, pronounced with unreleased /t/ or a final glottal stop, [kaʔ]. Of particular interest is a tendency to insert vowels (a phonological process known as epenthesis) between consonants to convert TL consonant clusters into a sequence of CV syllables, something that is uncharacteristic of child learners of English. Oller (1974a, 1974b) had argued that in L1 acquisition of phonology, it is most characteristic for learners under 3 years of age to simplify consonant clusters by reducing or deleting difficult consonants, as when they pronounced *blue* (CCV) as [bu] (CV). In contrast, L2 learners appeared to prefer epenthesis for this purpose; for example, adult L2 learners were shown to commonly insert a schwa vowel /ə/ into the consonant cluster /kl/ in the word *class* /klæs/, producing CVC /kəlæs/. They sometimes did this even to break up consonant clusters that also occurred in their NLs. In other words, NL transfer in phonology could be overridden in SLA by a preference for the unmarked CV syllable pattern achieved through the use of epenthesis (Tarone, 1980).

Developmental theories of SLA, while still focusing only on human cognition apart from social context, explicitly reject both explanations of habit-formation and the claim that humans are born with a specialized innate language-learning function. Rather, they argue that general cognitive processes can explain everything we observe in the development of learner language, including IL phonology. For example, Wode (1976, 1977) identified developmental sequences in German children's development of the English /ɹ/ that were similar to those observed in native English-speaking children, and that were apparently unaffected by German L1 transfer. Wode (1980) found that the English /ɹ/ was not difficult for L2 learners even though it does not exist in the NL. In other words, the forces of NL transfer in SLA could be overridden by a preference for more unmarked language forms, regardless of their presence or absence in the NL. Similarly, Processability Theory (Pienemann, 1998) argues that general cognitive constraints, such as ease or difficulty of changes in word order, can account for widespread developmental sequences in SLA. In the same way, this theory might argue that unmarked phonological features such as phonemes like /ɑ/ or syllable structures like the CV syllable are easier and earlier acquired because of general human physical and cognitive constraints, and not because of any innate biological capacity for language as Chomsky and others had proposed.

The alert reader may have noticed that bottom-up pedagogy for teaching L2 pronunciation is grounded on extensive research and teaching experience with highly literate and academically oriented post-secondary L2 learners who take a form-focused analytical approach to

SLA. However, in today's world, more and more L2 learners lack this kind of literacy and educational experience. Groups such as LESLLA (n.d.) have assembled a growing body of research on the way this population – which is mostly multilingual – acquires L2s (cf. Tarone, Bigelow, & Hansen, 2009). Specifically, there is growing evidence that print literacy – particularly alphabetic print literacy – has a significant impact on the cognitive processes of SLA upon which bottom-up viewpoints rely, such as the ability to notice corrective feedback on linguistic forms. Tarone (2021) reviews this evidence and suggests that, for populations of L2 learners with emergent literacy, a more top-down pedagogy may be preferable.

A Variationist Theory of SLA

Building on Hymes' (1972) construct of communicative competence, as well as others' work in this area, Canale and Swain (1980) proposed a theoretical model of L2 learners' communicative competence that went beyond the decontextualized grammatical competence that structuralist linguistics and cognitivist learning theories focused on. Learners' communicative competence as a focus of SLA research and teaching was to include not just grammatical competence but also sociolinguistic competence and strategic competence (e.g., communication strategies); the additional two kinds of competence had to take account of learners' use of their IL in social context. Drawing on research in sociolinguistics (e.g., Labov, 1970, 1972), variationist SLA researchers collected IL data from L2 learners engaged in social interactions – examining the impact of social contextual variables such as task, interlocutor, and social context on the linguistic forms L2 learners used in speaking – and found that those phonological and grammatical forms changed in response to such changing contextual variables.

Though Selinker's (1972) IL theory did not address the extent to which the IL rule system is affected when applied in social context, twelve years later, Selinker and Douglas (1985) – citing Tarone (1983), who posited on the basis of research (cited below) that IL systems varied in social context – provided a qualitative analysis of shifts in engineering graduate students' ILs in response to topic changes; they proposed that these learners had internalized an IL system made up of different varieties that were used in different discourse domains. Between 1972 and 1985, a group of SLA researchers had applied Labov's variationist sociolinguistic view of language use to IL data. They found that some parts of L2 learners' linguistic systems varied systematically in response to such social contextual factors as task constraints (L. Dickerson, 1975) and interlocutor (Beebe, 1977). They documented examples of shifts in interlanguage syntax (e.g., LoCoco, 1976; M. Schmidt, 1980; Tarone, 1985), morphology (e.g., Larsen-Freeman, 1975), and phonology (e.g., Beebe, 1980; L. Dickerson, 1975).

Tarone (1979) cited these studies as evidence that IL systems, like all human languages when used in human interaction, vary in response to shifts in various aspects of social context (task, topic, interlocutor), thus obeying Labov's (1970) classic "Observer's Paradox," which posited the following axioms among others:

Style-shifting

Every speaker shifts linguistic and phonetic variables as the social situation and topic change.

Attention

It is possible to range the styles of a speaker along a continuous dimension defined by the amount of attention paid to speech.

Vernacular

The vernacular style is produced when the least attention is paid to speech and exhibits more systematic phonological and grammatical patterns.

Formality

When a speaker pays more attention to speech, they produce a more formal style with phonology and grammar irregularly influenced by standard norms.

Studies of IL phonology in particular (summarized in Tarone, 1988) provided evidence that L2 learners' pronunciation patterns indeed obey the Observer's Paradox. IL phonology was shown to be systematically influenced particularly by the amount of attention to language production required by the task the L2 learner was asked to perform (Beebe, 1980; Dickerson & Dickerson, 1977; R. W. Schmidt, 1987) and by the ethnic identity of the interlocutor (Beebe, 1977, 1981). For example, Dickerson and Dickerson (1977) reported on Japanese learners who were given three tasks requiring them to produce English L2 consonant clusters containing /ɹ/: reading a list, reading a dialogue, and speaking spontaneously. Consistent with the Observers' Paradox, the learners produced the highest percentage of native-like /ɹ/ phonemes on the list-reading task which required more attention to form, a lower percentage of accurate /ɹ/ on the dialogue reading task, and the lowest percentage of accurate /ɹ/ on the free speech task which required least attention to form. Similarly, Beebe (1980) compared the impact of two tasks, reading a word list and conversation, on the use of several variants of syllable-initial and syllable-final R[1] in the IL phonology of nine adult Thai learners of English L2. In syllable-final position, the learners produced more accurate R in list-reading, and less accurate R in conversation. However, in syllable-initial position, this trend was reversed. A Thai variant /r/, a trilled R, considered a prestige accent in syllable-initial position in Thai, was used more frequently in syllable-initial position in the participants' careful English style (reading an English word list), while the American /ɹ/ was preferred in that position in their casual English style (conversation). Beebe (1977) also examined the impact of interlocutor on L2 learners' IL phonology; she analyzed nine vowels in the speech of 17 Chinese-Thai bilinguals as they were interviewed once by a Chinese interviewer and once by a Thai interviewer. The bilinguals used more Thai variants of those vowels with their Thai interviewer, and more Chinese variants with their Chinese interviewer.

Throughout this period, efforts were made to introduce theoretical explanations for variation in IL phonology in response to social context. Several of these will be described in more detail in Chapters 3 and 4, but they will be briefly outlined here. Guiora, Beit-Hallahmi, Brannon, Dull, and Scovel (1972) maintained that some L2 learners had more permeable ego boundaries that made them empathize with TL speakers; their IL phonology would then shift to conform to those speakers. Beebe and Giles (1984) proposed Speech Accommodation Theory to explain L2 learners' pronunciation shifts when addressing different interlocutors, suggesting that they tended to accommodate their pronunciation to more closely align with that of interlocutors they were drawn to, and to diverge from that of interlocutors they disliked. Tarone (1979, 1990) maintained that L2 learners' underlying IL phonological capability, or "knowledge," was itself variable and not homogeneous, and incorporated knowledge of social factors related to a range of styles. However, during the 20th century, efforts to theorize the learner's variable performance were not initially taken seriously by adherents of the three dominant theoretical paradigms (behaviorist, innatist, and cognitivist) in the field of SLA. As we shall see, it was not until the 21st century that Fasold and Preston (2007) offered a detailed visual model of a bilingual's grammar as a single mental construct with possible alternative realizations, in order to provide psycholinguistic validity to the notion of "variable rule."

Critical Period for Learning a Native-Like Accent

Regardless of theoretical orientation, an important issue in considering the acquisition of native-like pronunciation of an L2 is what has been termed the "critical period" (Lenneberg, 1967) for language learning. A vital question for researchers and teachers with a bottom-up orientation, given its focus on native-speaker accent as the goal, is whether that goal is even achievable by adults learning an L2. This is because there appears to be a critical period, or an age range "during which learners can acquire an L2 easily and achieve native-speaker competence, but... after this period L2 acquisition becomes more difficult and is rarely entirely successful" (Ellis, 2008, p. 259). Research appears to show that the goal of acquiring a native-like accent is almost impossible for adult L2 learners to attain. Scovel (1969) argued specifically that the critical period influences phonology much more than other linguistic areas (e.g., morphology, syntax, semantics); to support that claim, he pointed to individuals like Joseph Conrad, a highly successful English novelist who learned English after the critical period. Although Conrad became a master of English syntax and semantics, his Polish accent persisted his entire life. Other illustrative examples like Henry Kissinger, former Secretary of State and U.S. politician of German origins, also come to mind. In fact, it appears that while children who undergo normal cognitive development appear to effortlessly become completely successful in pronouncing their NL perfectly, L2 learners who have aged out of the critical period appear to be unable to do so. Indeed, Scovel (personal communication to Tarone, 1981) even suggested that it was cruel for pronunciation teachers to tell their adult students they could produce native-like accents if they just tried harder – as cruel as telling them they could fly if they just flapped their arms hard enough.

Why is it so difficult for adults to learn to pronounce an L2 in a native-like way, "without an accent?" Different possible causes for the critical period for pronunciation in SLA have been proposed. Explanations range from some learners' beliefs that the muscles in their tongues needed to produce unfamiliar TL segments have atrophied with age, to Scovel's (1969, 1988) hypothesis that the cause is physical changes in the brain, specifically, the lateralization of brain function that occurs with maturation. Long (1990) also traced the cause of the critical period to brain maturation, but he pointed to a different kind of brain function – in this case, a progressive loss of neural plasticity possibly associated with increasing myelination.

Most innatist SLA researchers have argued that the critical period for language acquisition occurs because sometime before adolescence, the individual loses full access to the innate biological cognitive capacity for language. It is this capacity that enables the learner to achieve a native-like accent. While some researchers, such as Krashen (1981, 1982), have maintained that adult L2 learners can completely reactivate the same innate and universal cognitive processes they once used to acquire their L1s, most UG researchers take a more moderate position, suggesting that after adolescence, adults have less access to the innate capacity for language learning. The extent and nature of this loss of access has continued to be a matter of debate, with different UG SLA scholars taking different positions. Some linguists (beginning with Selinker, 1972, and even including Chomsky, 1988) believe that the biological capacity for language learning essentially ends after the critical period, since we observe dramatic differences in process and outcomes between child L1 acquisition and adult L2 acquisition. Selinker (1972) for example points out that while all children who undergo normal cognitive development successfully acquire their NL and attain perfect competence (including perfect native accents), few to no comparable adults achieve that same outcome in acquiring an L2. Based on such divergent outcomes, he reasons that having passed through the critical period, adults must engage different general cognitive capacities and processes in SLA, unlike children acquiring their NL. This change in access to UG prevents adults' attainment of native-like TL accents as well as the formation of ILs that obey all of the language universals that characterize native languages.

As Tarone (1990) observes, even Chomsky, the initiator of generative linguistic theory, pointed to clear cognitive differences between L1 acquisition, which engages innate biological forces, and adult L2 acquisition, which is influenced by social forces. He says that since the innate full biological capacity for language learning probably ends in childhood, "for the language teacher, that means that you simply cannot teach a language to an adult the way a child learns a language" (Chomsky, 1988, p. 179). He goes on to say that social context is the difference and must be taken into account in an adequate explanation for SLA since in using two languages "... somehow the brain must have simultaneously several different switch settings. Now it appears that this is possible only when somehow the [human]... associates each language with a certain kind of situation" (Chomsky, 1998, p. 188).

Chomsky's statement is consistent with variationist SLA theory, which as we have noted did not fit the more dominant cognitivist and generative learning theories of the 20th century. Variationists had their own explanation for the critical period for L2 learning. For example, Tarone (1988), citing Guiora et al. (1972), argued that the cause was likely to be socio-emotional in nature, in that children might be more willing than most adults to empathize with other speakers, taking on their identities in language play and adopting pronunciation patterns like theirs, while adults' more defined ego boundaries might cause them to resist that level of empathy and pronunciation shift (Tarone, 1988, pp. 82–83).

Field-Specific Language: A Growing Focus on Intelligibility

Beginning in the 1970's, increasing numbers of international students enrolled in U.S. universities in a wide range of disciplines, but particularly in math, science, and engineering; in their departments, international graduate students were increasingly hired as Teaching Assistants, positions requiring them to use English, their L2, to teach introductory classes in their chosen disciplines to American undergraduates. It quickly became clear to their students, teachers, and program administrators alike that such International Teaching Assistants (ITAs) often struggled to communicate this critical information to their students. In this context, the goal of native-speaker accent was quickly subsumed by the goal of intelligibility; what mattered to their students (and their concerned parents) was not so much whether their teachers spoke with a North American English accent, as whether they could clearly transmit disciplinary content to their charges.

As we have seen, during this period, in so-called "general" English as a Second Language (ESL) programs for international students, there was still a bottom-up emphasis on native-like accent as the primary goal of typical pronunciation courses. However, it appears there was dwindling interest in such courses; Anderson-Hsieh (1990), for example, cited diminished interest in pronunciation, possibly due to a disenchantment with traditional methods of teaching pronunciation, which emphasized segmentals and drilling of minimal pairs of sounds. Research on ITAs conducted by Hinofotis and Bailey (1981) argued for a more practical goal and methodology. According to Levis (2018, pp. 13–14), Hinofotis and Bailey found that even though some ITAs had advanced language proficiency and expertise in course content, their students still found them hard to understand; these researchers argued for a rethinking of the dichotomy between native and native-like accent and concluded that what ITAs needed was some threshold level of skill in pronunciation to improve their intelligibility.

In writing about this period, Levis (2018) underscores the importance of ITA work in the way that pronunciation was viewed in the wider context. He states:

> It is hard to underestimate the importance of ITA work in the changing role of pronunciation, and the research done with ITAs went hand in hand with many of the changes in L2 pronunciation teaching... The proposal that learners who could not become native-like could become more intelligible was part of a broader change in how pronunciation became relevant again. (Levis, 2018, pp. 219–220)

Textbooks such as Byrd, Constantinides, and Pennington (1989) and Pica, Gregory, and Finger (1990), which were designed for ITA courses during this period, illustrate these courses' pedagogical focus on intelligibility in oral discourse. Standing in stark contrast to the continuing bottom-up method of teaching pronunciation that prevailed at the time in "general ESL" courses (and also the concurrent bottom-up orientation to SLA pronunciation research), such textbooks provide an instructive example of the growing undercurrent of the top-down orientation in ITA courses, necessarily due to these learners' pragmatic communicative needs. We will illustrate this new top-down approach by focusing on one such textbook, Smith, Meyers, and Burkhalter (1992), *Communicate: Strategies for International Teaching Assistants.* The authors based the book on a tripartite framework for preparing international graduate students to function as Teaching Assistants in U.S. universities: language (pronunciation and vocabulary), teaching, and culture. To shed light on our recommendation that language be taught in relation to intelligibility, we will address it from two different aspects: (1) Intelligibility and Suprasegmentals and (2) Field-Specific Vocabulary.

Intelligibility and Suprasegmentals

What aspects of pronunciation should be taught to improve intelligibility? When undergraduates were asked about their ITAs' pronunciation difficulties, they complained more about suprasegmentals – intonation, stress, linking, rhythm, and fluency – than segmentals (cf. S. Stevens,

1989, p. 182). According to Anderson-Hsieh (1990), experts in ESL at the time were agreeing that "suprasegmentals are more critical for intelligibility than segmentals" (p. 200), citing the writings of W. Dickerson (1989), Gilbert (1987), Pennington and Richards (1986), and Wong (1987). As Levis (2018) concludes in his retrospective on this period, ITAs' need to produce longer stretches of oral discourse in explaining their disciplines to their students also prioritized suprasegmentals: "Unlike segmentals, suprasegmentals were an easier fit with approaches that placed importance on fluent productions of longer stretches of speech (discourse)" (Levis, 2018, p. 199).

If we examine *Communicate*'s Table of Contents, we see that the initial diagnostic pronunciation test consists of a contextualized paragraph containing sentences that require pausing for meaning and a variety of question types that require attention to final intonation patterns. The diagnostic checklist that is provided contains only one section for segmentals; the remaining areas focus on suprasegmentals and fluency. The language portions of the text move from word stress through thought groups, to connected speech (reduction, linking, and rhythm), and on to intonation (final intonation and primary sentence stress). Segmentals are only covered at the very end in the chapters on enunciation and *-ed* and *-s* endings.

Field-Specific Vocabulary

In addition to the textbook's emphasis on suprasegmental aspects of pronunciation for intelligibility, *Communicate* was the first book of its kind to include visuals, terms, passages, questions, general interest topics, and problems from a total of 15 academic fields ranging from engineering to sociology. In doing this, the textbook heeds Anderson-Hsieh's (1990, p. 195) strong argument for having ITAs focus on field-specific terms and vocabulary for pronunciation development "based on the students' pronunciation needs and intelligibility considerations." As Levis (2018) points out:

> Many ITAs have difficulty with the spoken forms of key vocabulary, and rather than systematic pronunciation instruction, are taught to pronounce the key disciplinary and academic vocabulary needed to communicate in academic contexts. ... This approach to vocabulary learning, which is inspired by the English for Specific Purposes movement, may be quite important in an intelligibility–based approach. (pp. 244–245)

Learning to correctly stress and intelligibly pronounce key terms makes much more sense in a time-dependent curriculum than spending time on general pronunciation of the vocabulary of English. For example, the chapter in *Communicate* which focuses on word stress introduces ITAs to the field-specific vocabulary that they will need to use in their classrooms and provides opportunities for them to practice these terms in isolation and later, in context.

Thus, during the 1980's, even as SLA research and "general" L2 pronunciation classes continued to use a bottom-up orientation in the study and teaching of pronunciation, there was a growing undercurrent of research and pedagogy employing a top-down view of the study and teaching of oral discourse, including pronunciation, in ITA courses as well as other Language for Specific Purposes courses. During the 1990's, a growing conflict between these two orientations broke the surface in mainstream L2 research and teaching, during a period of debate over the role of communicative context that came to be known as the "SLA Wars."

The "SLA Wars" over Variation in IL

The bottom-up cognitive structuralist orientation of SLA researchers made good progress in many ways during the 20th century with its focus on decontextualized linguistic forms of both IL and TL phonology, but these researchers did not seriously consider the impact of either the significance of those forms to the learner or the impact of interaction or social context on their use and development of IL systems. Structuralist, innatist researchers like Gregg (1990) simply asserted, but never demonstrated, that social context had no impact on the development of IL phonology, which was conceptualized as idealized, decontextualized competence; innatists argued that social context affected performance, but never competence. However, increasingly, questions were raised about the decontextualized study of L2 learners' IL phonology and grammar, and more SLA scholars began to call for top-down research incorporating social context and social identity. For example, as we shall see below, these researchers began to question whether the goal of pronunciation instruction should be restricted to acquisition of a native-speaker accent. They pointed to the low levels of success adults had in reaching that goal, and in some cases, they began to argue that it might be more important for the L2 learner to focus on intelligibility – whether interlocutors could understand their pronunciation.

Some also stressed the *emic* meaning of a foreign vs. native accent to the learner, that is, the psychosocial meaning of an accent to the learner (see Pike's, 1967, distinction between *emic* and *etic* meaning). They wondered how a learner's choice among different accents might be influenced by social contextual factors like interlocutor, task (e.g., role-play or storytelling), or situational formality. As shown above on page 13, Selinker himself came to notice that each L2 learner's interlanguage was produced differentially as they spoke about different topics such as performing different roles in different social contexts. For example, Selinker and Douglas (1985) described international graduate students who were observed to speak more fluently and accurately use more complex grammatical and lexical constructions when lecturing about their discipline than when chatting informally about how to cook something. They postulated that L2 learners' acquisition processes were affected by these internally defined different IL discourse domains.

The "SLA Wars" in the 1990's – a conflict between bottom-up and top-down researchers about the role of social context in SLA in shaping the development of IL linguistic systems as compared to TL systems – marked the beginning of the end of this period of complete dominance of bottom-up models. Gregg (1990) initiated an attack on the variationist theories of SLA listed earlier on in this chapter, and specifically Tarone's (1983) model of IL as a capability continuum and Ellis' (1985) variable competence model. Gregg accurately stated that these related views of L2 learners' underlying IL, and indeed all variationist theories, were a rejection of the distinction between competence and performance and therefore a rejection of the principles of generative grammar and the SLA theories based on those principles. Even while conceding that phonology is most likely to exhibit variation, Gregg offered the generative argument that a learner's language knowledge – which is by definition ideal and so cannot vary – and their language output – which is variable – are completely distinct. Responses by Tarone (1990) and Ellis (1990) were invited by the journal editor and defended the necessity of incorporating an L2 learner's knowledge of social contextual variables into that learner's IL knowledge system.

During this decade, others also took up the variationist argument. Rampton (1995) argued that a decontextualized bottom-up cognitive orientation focused so much on analyzing learner language for evidence of "psycholinguistic states and processes" (p. 293) that it completely missed the way learner language could be shaped by the learner's social negotiation of identity in oral interactions:

The very undifferentiated portrait of the second language learner that emerges in SLA no doubt partly results from its tendency to thematise the learner's internal psychological condition. Rather than looking at interaction as a socio-historically sensitive arena in which language learner identity is socially negotiated, SLA generally examines learner behaviour for evidence of the determining influence of psycholinguistic states and processes. (Rampton, 1995, p. 293)

In a widely cited article, Firth and Wagner (1997) argued that SLA research had become imbalanced, with too much emphasis on cognitive-oriented theories and methodologies focused on knowledge about language, and too little emphasis on social and interaction-oriented theories and methodologies focused on language use. Firth and Wagner called for three changes in the field of SLA, all of which we would view as initiating a more top-down perspective; they called for:

1) more study of the contextual and interactional dimensions of language use;
2) a focus on a more emic dimension of phonology (i.e., the psychosocial meaning of accent to the learner); and
3) an expansion of the data base upon which SLA research relies, to include participants' interactive encounters with interlocutors in a wider range of social roles and contexts and for a wider range of purposes.

In critiquing the bottom-up, cognitivist structuralist orientation to SLA research, Firth and Wagner (1997, p. 285) say:

SLA research takes a view of the learner that is too individualistic and mechanistic, and... fails to account in a satisfactory way for interactional and sociolinguistic dimensions of language. As such, it is flawed, and obviates insight into the nature of language, most centrally the language use of second or foreign language (S/FL) speakers.

In response to such critiques, researchers with a cognitivist structuralist orientation presented forceful arguments that social context had absolutely no impact on SLA; rather, SLA should be conceived of as an entirely internal psychological process. Memorably, Long (1998) issued this challenge:

Remove a learner from the social setting, and the L2 grammar does not change or disappear. Change the social setting altogether, e.g., from street to classroom, or from a foreign to a second language environment, and, as far as we know, the way the learner acquires does not change much either, as suggested, e.g., by comparisons of error types, developmental sequences, processing constraints, and other aspects of the acquisition process in and out of classrooms.... (p. 93)

Tarone (2000) took up Long's challenge that no such research evidence existed. She cited years of variationist research showing that social factors do impact several of the psychological processes of SLA listed by Long (1998), including acquisition processes, error monitoring, and developmental sequences. Among the works she cited in response to Long's challenge were Bondevik (1996), Kormos (1999), Liu (1991), and Tarone and Liu (1995). Bondevik (1996), for example, demonstrates that different interlocutors outside of academia provided L2 learners with very different amounts of negotiation of meaning and adjusted TL input (both major drivers of SLA according to Long). Kormos (1999, p. 330) shows that L2 learners' awareness of and monitoring of their own errors shifted with different interlocutors in different social contexts. Most notably, addressing the relationship between social context and IL developmental sequences, Liu (1991) and Tarone and Liu (1995) show that the developmental sequence of English questions of an L2 learner were altered by the learner's participation in interactions with different interlocutors. Tarone (2000) concluded that Long's categorical rejection of a consideration of social context as an influence on psychological processes of SLA could not stand. While bottom-up studies might have a role to play, it was clear that in refusing to consider the role of context and learner identity in learners' efforts to acquire native-like linguistic systems, they were throwing out the baby with the bathwater.

Major's (2001) influential book offers a way out of the SLA wars that focuses specifically on IL phonology. It provides an extensive review of scholarship and research on foreign accent and IL phonology, including both bottom-up and some newer top-down perspectives in L2 pronunciation research on both segmental and prosodic aspects. The book title, *Foreign Accent*, makes clear Major's focus on an IL phonology that differs from a TL phonology. In other words, the book focuses on the learning goal of native-like pronunciation, and not on intelligibility.

Major (2001) shows that almost all of this research acknowledges the role of both language transfer from the NL and language universals in forming IL phonology (foreign accent). In addition, he concludes that although variation studies in SLA were relatively recent at the time, any "encompassing theory of SLA" had to include an account of variation (Major, 2001, p. 79). Major improves on Tarone (1988) in documenting the major impact of social context and social factors upon L2 learners' acquisition, competence, and use of IL phonology, concluding that "... any model, theory, or purported explanation that fails to account for variation is not accounting for the data, period" (p. 69). In this, he refers to learners' IL phonology as a linguistic system that shifts and systematically varies as learners interact in different social contexts, such as with different interlocutors, or performing more or less formal oral speaking tasks. Indeed, Major's Ontogeny Phylogeny Model of phonological acquisition predicts that, no matter what the analyst's linguistic theory, the same factors – language transfer, L2 acquisition processes, and universal constraints – all will be found to combine to shape an IL phonological competence that is itself variable. Major concludes that all linguistic systems are inherently subject to both diachronic change over time and synchronous stylistic variation.

Besides accounting for inevitable variation, Major also stresses the importance of learner identity and the emic dimension of phonology – the psychosocial meaning of accent to the learner – which is something that is completely missing in bottom-up orientations that focus only on decontextualized structuralist descriptions: "A person's NL accent is part of one's sense of identity and personality. Identity and personality can affect L2 accent, and in turn L2 accent can affect identity and personality. These traits are inexorably intertwined with social factors" (Major, 2001, p. 66). As Major shows, asking a learner to accurately produce TL phonemes and TL prosody is not just a mechanical matter of changing NL habits or struggling to produce a relatively difficult phoneme high on the markedness hierarchy. Rather, at a deeper psychosocial level, it is asking L2 learners to redefine themselves as having a new identity or personality, or to come across as persons embedded in, for example, French culture and values rather than as, for example, Americans embedded in an Upper Midwestern culture with Midwestern values. The study of L2 pronunciation forces the L2 learner to ask, *Do I really want to sound like I'm French when I'm really an American?*

Chapter 2 in Review

In this chapter, we have reviewed bottom-up research on IL phonology and pronunciation that predominated in the second half of the 20th century, and the growing amount of top-down scholarship and research initiated towards the close of that century. We characterized the orientation to language taken in bottom-up SLA research on pronunciation as structuralist, focusing on the physical and linguistic forms of the stream of speech in isolation from the social context of speaking, that is, on its linguistic segments (phonemes), rules for producing these in connected speech, and rules for the prosodic features of intonation, stress, and rhythm. In this structuralist orientation, the linguistic target in learning L2 phonology is assumed to be the standard accent of a NS of the L2, and L2 pronunciation learning is treated as a completely mental process that is unaffected by social context.

In describing the bottom-up cognitivist orientation to learning, we reviewed and compared three major cognitivist theories of SLA: behaviorist, innatist, and developmental. The initially less-influential variationist theory of SLA began with the discovery of problems with cognitivism in research on IL phonology. The first was that L2 learners' phonological forms and rules systematically varied when they performed different types of speaking tasks; the second was that those forms and rules also varied when L2 learners interacted with different interlocutors. Social context was increasingly harder for some researchers to dismiss. Research on the efforts of L2 learners to emulate the accents of idealized NSs also produced growing evidence that there was a critical period for success; while children were shown to succeed fairly easily, adults almost universally failed to achieve a native-like accent. Bottom-up researchers debated the causes of this fossilization in the development of IL phonology, attributing it primarily to either the physical development of the brain or to identified stages of cognitive development; variationist researchers suggested that accent signals ethnic and emotional identity, which is less permeable for adults than for children.

As mainstream research on IL phonology struggled with issues arising from their bottom-up view of language and learning and their focus on native-like accent as a goal, a small body of research focused on a specialized group of L2 learners – international graduate students in U.S. universities whose efforts to teach undergraduates were being undercut by pronunciation difficulties. Early on, these researchers observed that the problem was not that these L2 learners lacked a native-like accent; it was that their speech was not intelligible to their audience. In researching what makes speech intelligible, these scholars identified not just specific phonemes, but prosodic features like intonation, stress, and rhythm in relation to the information structure of lectures, in coordination with non-verbal features[2] such as gesture, pausing, and use of space in interaction with an audience. In this way, this group of researchers began to diverge from the orientation underlying bottom-up research on IL phonology.

These developments culminated in the so-called "SLA Wars" of the 1990's, a conflict between researchers insisting on the validity of bottom-up research on SLA, which explicitly rejected the study of the impact of social context on the learning process, and variationist and ITA researchers, whose results showed that social context and situational factors had a systematic impact on learners' acquisition of an L2. They argued that a pronunciation accent as a symbol of social identity had a defining impact on a learner's success, and that IL phonology was clearly variable when used intentionally by learners to project a desired role or identity in their social interactions.

Chapter 2 Notes

1. Beebe (1980) states, "Capital letters are used as names for phonological variables. ...They are symbols of socially conditioned variables and do not have a single phonetic realization, but rather a continuum of phonetic realizations. For example, the name R represents a phonological variable in Thai which may be realized phonetically as a flap, a trill, or a lateral continuant" (p. 435).
2. In subsequent chapters, we will refer to non-verbal features such as gesture, pausing, and use of space as *non-verbals*.

Chapter 3

Top-Down Research on Interlanguage Phonology

Orientation to Language and Learning

Top-down research and teaching of L2 pronunciation rejects "native accent" as the goal of learning and instruction, replacing it with two related but distinct learning goals:

1) intelligibility; and
2) a TL accent that expresses the learner's identity.

As we showed in Chapter 2, some top-down research on IL phonology was done during a period when bottom-up research was in the ascendancy, but it was essentially ignored by proponents of behaviorism, innatism, and cognitivism because it did not fit their dominant paradigm. However, at the end of the SLA Wars of the 1990's (just recounted), there was a paradigm shift in the field, sometimes referred to as the "Social Turn in SLA" (Block, 2003), in which many top-down practitioners joined ITA instructors in deciding that the goal of a native-like accent should be abandoned. This was in part because of the general paradigm shift and in part because SLA research had established that almost no adult L2 learners could achieve a native accent. Instead, researchers and teachers argued for the more practical and achievable goal of intelligibility – could L2 users speak so as to be easily understood by their interlocutors? At the same time, the social turn to top-down practice included more focus on learner agency in oral interactions, leading to a shift to the realization that L2 learners could select as a goal TL accents with particular emic, or personal, significance. In oral interactions, adult L2 learners might favor non-native-like accents that better express their evolving identities and cultural allegiances. In the following sections, we will explore in detail top-down research addressing these two goals: intelligibility and accent as identity.

Intelligibility as Speaking Goal

As noted in Chapter 1, we use the term *intelligibility*, broadly defined, to refer to whether "listeners can understand the speaker's message" (Derwing & Munro, 2015, p. 1); obviously, intelligibility relies heavily on the perception of the interlocutor with whom the L2 speaker interacts. As shown in Chapter 2, much of the consensus on intelligibility as a major goal of pronunciation instruction initially arose out of the need to improve the communication skills of ITAs in U.S. colleges and universities who were given jobs teaching introductory courses to undergraduates in virtually all major disciplines. Even when the bottom-up method of teaching pronunciation was in its ascendancy, practitioners assisting ITAs with their speaking skills had decided that, for their unique purposes, the goal of instruction should be intelligibility and not NS accent. If ITAs still had a "foreign accent" but were intelligible, they could do their jobs; the opposite was clearly not the case. What mattered was their ability to be clear and otherwise communicatively effective in transmitting basic disciplinary information to students through the medium of English, their L2. Research on aspects of IL phonology most crucial for ITAs' intelligibility in university teaching contexts expanded to many other teaching contexts after the Social Turn.

Although the area of ITA education initially led the way, other research has identified similar issues supporting the development of intelligibility in a range of social contexts outside of university-level ITA education, particularly in workplaces in Canada and Australia. For example, Munro et al. (2006) asked English-speaking listeners from different native language backgrounds (Mandarin, Cantonese, Japanese, and English) to rate the intelligibility, comprehensibility, and accentedness of the English of non-native speakers whose NLs were Catalan, Japanese, Polish, and Spanish. The different NL groups gave the speakers very similar ratings on intelligibility, comprehensibility, and accentedness, with no apparent preference given to speakers whose NL was the same as that of the rater. There was wide agreement on who was easiest and most difficult to understand.

Derwing and Munro (2009) then reported research on the accentedness and comprehensibility of spontaneous English speech samples provided by 10 native speakers of Mandarin and 10 native speakers of Slavic languages. These samples were rated for accentedness and comprehensibility, and for overall preferability by workers from petrochemical companies, most of them engineers. Results showed that for these workers, higher ratings for preferability corresponded with higher ratings for comprehensibility rather than for accentedness. Based on these and more detailed results, the researchers recommended training for both speakers and listeners in the workplace, providing detailed suggestions regarding such training.

Derwing, Munro, Foote, Waugh, and Fleming (2014) went on to report on the results of a successful pronunciation training program in a window company in Canada that was provided for seven English L2 workers who had lived in an English-speaking environment for an average of 19 years and were perceived as having fossilized pronunciation. Considerable detail is provided on the curriculum and instruction provided to the workers; it included both perception and production of segments and prosodic elements of English. After a 17-hour intervention (34 classes) over a period of three months, based on results of pre- and post-intervention tests rated by 28 native speakers of English, the explicit instruction was shown to produce significant improvement in the participants' comprehensibility, intelligibility, and perception, though, interestingly, not in accent or fluency.

Finally, Derwing (2016) reviews and describes research on English L2 engineers in their workplaces that shows that immigrants' comprehensibility was affected by three factors: pronunciation, pragmatics, and proficiency. For example, a training course that included both pronunciation and pragmatics produced improved comprehensibility while a course that focused only on pronunciation did not.

Based on this and related research, there is now considerable agreement on the aspects of communication L2 learners need to change to improve their intelligibility. This research suggests that the solution requires a focus on what Yates (2017) calls *delivery* – a combination of:

- pronunciation (segments in connected speech; word and utterance stress focused on meaning; and intonation, including pitch/key);
- non-verbals (gaze, gesture, stance[1], proxemics); and
- pragmatics (speech acts, softeners, directness).

In what follows, we review research on each of these features that improve intelligibility.

Prosody

Research has clearly established that listener-defined intelligibility is closely tied to the speaker's ability to master the prosody of the L2

– particularly the placement of prominence in a sentence and the use of pitch height and rising tones in intonation (Hahn, 2004; Kang, Rubin, & Pickering, 2010; Pickering, 2001). Pickering (2012) defines intonation as "the systematic and linguistically meaningful use of pitch movement at the phrasal or suprasegmental level" (p. 280). The term *suprasegmental* substantially overlaps with the term *prosody*, which is defined as a combination of pitch movement, syllable length, and loudness (Pennington & Ellis, 2000).

Research on the discourse of ESL learners has found that they have considerable difficulty with intonation. Pirt (1990) found that Italian learners of English struggled to master intonation to signal information in oral discourse. Similarly, Wennerstrom (1994) focused on discourse-level intonation; she compared the recorded oral readings and free speech of Japanese, Thai, and Chinese learners of English and NSs of English with respect to intonational meaning (the relative prominence of the words in an utterance and the pitch configuration at phrase boundaries). The most striking finding involved the NSs' use of a substantial pitch increase to signal new information, as opposed to information that was assumed to be mutually understood. Another was that the Japanese and Thai NSs used low, falling tones at phrase boundaries where the Spanish and English NSs used rising or mid-level tones. The author suggests that L2 speakers who are not aware of such intonational cues might misunderstand important aspects of NS discourse.

Hewings (1995) studied the English discourse of 12 advanced-level learners – four each from Korea, Greece, and Indonesia – in comparison with that of 12 NSs of British English. The NS and non-native speaker (NNS) groups were recorded reading the same dialogue, and differences between the tone choices of the two groups were identified. Hewings analyzed their intonation using Brazil's (1985/1997) model of discourse intonation, which assumes that tone choices are made in oral discourse where speakers and hearers assume a shared and ever-changing context of understandings called *common ground*. A rising tone marks information assumed to be shared common ground, whereas a falling tone marks a new addition to common ground. Results showed that when communicating varying levels of lack of agreement (contradicting a previous speaker, withholding agreement with the speaker, and expressing reservations), all of the NNSs overused falling tones, while the NSs of British English used rising tones for purposes which Hewings labeled "social integration." For example, when contradicting a previous speaker, where NNSs used a falling tone, the NSs always used a rising tone in order to avoid communicating overt disagreement, assuming a falling tone might communicate animosity or rudeness in situations where none was intended.

Pennington and Ellis (2000) compare prosody in English (an intonation language) and Cantonese (a tone language) in order to understand the difficulties Cantonese learners have in mastering prosody in English as an L2. In Cantonese, prosody is a cue to meaning at the lexical level, while in English prosody cues meaning at the phrase, clause, and discourse levels. Thus, Cantonese speakers have to overcome NL transfer to learn that English intonation is distributed across entire clauses and even sentences, and that contrasting prosodic patterns across these units can change their meaning. Pennington and Ellis' research study established that 30 Cantonese learners of English did indeed have great difficulty distinguishing between the meanings of English sentence pairs in which the words were identical, but where prosodic prominence was either unmarked or marked, such as:

> Is he driving the bus? (unmarked; no special emphasis or contrast)
> Is HE driving the bus? (marked; focus on HE for contrast or emphasis)

The researchers examined the learners' responses to such sentence pairs both when the contrastive focus was implicit and when it was the explicit focus of attention. Results showed first, that in the implicit condition, the participants focused on the meaning of the words but treated prosody indications of contrast between such sentences as incidental; for them, both sentences had the same meaning. After explicit priming focused on prosodic contrasts of meaning, there was only marginal change; the participants still had great difficulty comprehending prosody, especially for more marked types of prosodic contrast at the clause, sentence, and discourse levels.

In a related study, Reed and Michaud (2015) also demonstrated that L2 learners were unable to discern underlying meanings that were signaled by marked intonation. The learners were shown sentence pairs where the stress in the second sentence includes a fall-rise contour indicating an implicit contrast, such as:

> The teacher didn't grade your papers.
> The TEACHER didn't grade your papers.

When shown such sentences, the learners stated they believed both sentences meant the same thing. For them, words were more important than intonation when they processed English speech.

Kang et al. (2010) found that such prosodic aspects of L2 speech accounted for 50% of the variance in listeners' ratings of intelligibility. The specific ways in which suprasegmentals impact intelligibility in authentic oral discourse (such as that of ITAs) has recently been documented by research in two areas: the role of intonation in marking the information structure of extended discourse, and the synchronous relationship in oral discourse of prosody and non-verbal elements such as gesture, eye gaze, and head movement.

Work with ITAs has shown that prosody and suprasegmentals play an important role, both in signaling a lecture's information structure and in establishing rapport with an audience. Pickering (2001) uses Brown's framework of discourse analysis (Brown, 1977; Brown & Yule, 1983), and Brazil's (1985/1997) model of intonation to compare NS and NNS lectures in English-medium classrooms. She finds that a major obstacle to NNS oral communication is tone choice: that is, whether the pitch movement on the tonic syllable is rising, falling, or level. The NSs in this study systematically exploited tone choice by using both rising and falling tone choices, depending on whether they were reminding students of shared information using a rising tone or telling them new information by using a falling tone. While NSs systematically exploited tone choice to increase the accessibility of discourse content to students and improve rapport, the NNSs' tonal composition interfered with the information structure of their discourse and also caused students to view them as unsympathetic, due to their overuse of falling tone choices, leading students to feel their instructors were telling them information which they already knew.

The following example from Gorsuch, Meyers, Pickering, and Griffee (2013) illustrates a NS teaching assistant's tone choices to highlight information structure while establishing rapport. In this example, the stressed syllable of the last prominent word (indicated in capital letters) is underlined and the direction of the tone (falling ⬎; rising ⬈; or level ➜) is indicated with a thick arrow immediately before the tonic syllable in the thought group.

> now of course you reMEMber from Dr. Wilson's lecture that potassium was ⬈PURple // gave a purple or a ⬈VIolet flame // today you MIGHT see that as ⬎WELL // and the THIRD possibility is that there will be no color at ⬎ALL (Gorsuch et al., 2013, p. 43)

Each thought group in the discourse contains one or more prominent words which the speaker deems important. In the excerpt above, the NS Teaching Assistant considers the words *remember, purple, violet, might, well*, *third*, and *all* as important to the information structure. The stressed syllable in the last prominent word in the thought group (*purple*, *violet*, *well*, and *all*) is the one that receives the tone choice, that is, the most salient and sustained pitch movement. The words *purple* and *violet* use rising tones; the speaker considers this shared information. On the other hand, *well* and *all* use falling tones, indicating that the speaker considers the information in these two thought groups to be new information for the students. Thus, the speaker's use of rising tones on the words *purple* and *violet* build rapport with the audience by acknowledging their prior knowledge while the use of falling tones on *well* and *all* offer them expectations for the experiment they are about to do.

Compare this to the tone choices of a NNS ITA in the following example from Pickering (2001):

> // the FIRST ↘ STEP // you do is FLAME ↘ TEST // for ↘SOdium ion // if YOU have ↘SOdium ion // you will get BIG yellow Orange // but if you↘ HAVEn't // there will be →NO // BIG yellow ↘Orange (p. 248)

The ITA above knows his audience has already conducted one set of flame tests, but his level and falling tone choices (instead of the rising tone choices the NS teaching assistant used) do not acknowledge this, but rather present the information as if it is entirely new to them. These choices fail to mark discourse structure clearly and also negatively affect rapport with his audience.

An earlier example of the importance of tone choice comes from Gumperz' (1982) description of how the unexpected intonation pattern of Indian and Pakistani workers in an airport cafeteria in Britain caused them to be perceived as "surly and uncooperative" by the British English-speaking interlocutors. To ask a British cargo handler if he wanted gravy with his meat, a British English-speaking worker would say "↗gravy" using rising intonation. In this situation, the Indian English speakers said "↘gravy" using a falling intonation; thus, their offer was actually perceived to be a demand by the British English-speaking interlocutors.

To show the role of prosody and suprasegmentals in signaling the information structure of oral discourse, Brazil (1985/1997) proposes a paragraph unit of intonation. Intonation paragraphs are sections of a talk containing a main point. According to Pickering (2018), acoustically we can identify an intonation paragraph in the following way:

> ... the boundaries of these units are produced and interpreted using phonetic cues. The most prominent cues include a high pitch onset (high key) with an accelerated rate and volume and a low pitch close

(low termination) possibly accompanied by a drop in volume and narrowing of the pitch range. (p. 62)

The following example, provided by Gorsuch et al. (2013) and taken from a chemistry lab, illustrates this. In this transcript, the upward arrows (↑) indicate high key, and the downward arrows (↓) indicate low key.

> A ↑COUple of things real quick about the safety video. If you come across a mercury thermometer it is a lot more difficult to get those cleaned up if it breaks. A haz-mat crew has to come out and get it cleaned up. So, if you come across a mercury thermometer in here just let me know and we'll put it ↓aSIDE.

> As ↑FAR as finishing your safety quiz, the fire extinguishers are in the hall. The MSDS sheets are located in room one eleven, which is the help room right next door. The eye wash stations are at the end of each one of the benches here. I just checked 'em and they all ↓WORK. (Gorsuch et al., 2013, p. 69)

Changes in pitch identify two speech paragraphs in the chemistry talk. The high pitch reset at the start of the second paragraph is a clear cue to the change in topic. The first intonation paragraph or topic focuses on a safety video which students have just viewed, and the second one addresses information that students will need to complete a safety quiz which they have been given. If we were to illustrate this phenomenon visually using speech software, it would look something like this:

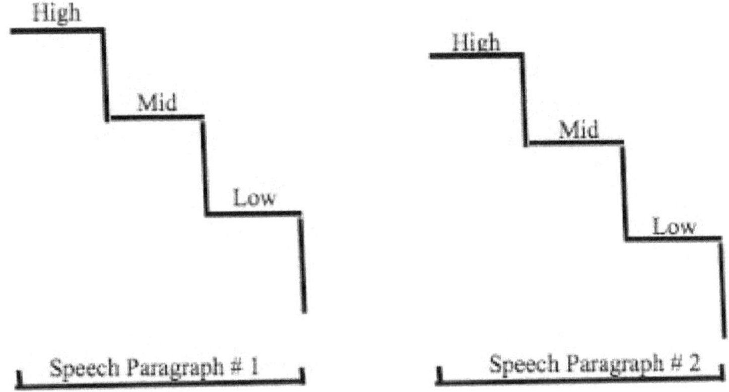

FIGURE 3.1. Illustration of Key Choice in Intonation Paragraphs
(Figure 1, Gorsuch et al., 2013, p. 62. Reprinted by permission of Waveland Press, Inc., from Gorsuch, Greta; Meyers, Colleen; Pickering, Lucy, & Griffee, Dale T., *English Communication for International Teaching Assistants*, Second Edition. Long Grove, IL: Waveland Press, Inc. ©2013. All rights reserved.)

NNS lecturers have difficulty producing such clear intonation paragraphs due to a compressed pitch range and a much lower initial pitch at the beginning of each paragraph, as well as shorter pauses at paragraph boundaries. Focusing markers such as *for the first part* or *first off* used by NNSs within these paragraphs are also much less prosodically distinct, making it more difficult for listeners to identify key information in the lecture. Pickering's work makes it very clear why ITAs need to master English prosody to make their lectures more intelligible to their students. Generally speaking, such findings crucially reinforce the importance of intonation in social discourse to communicate information comprehensibly and intelligibly, and to build rapport with interlocutors.

Non-Verbal Communication

Research has also shown that non-verbal communication such as gaze, gesture, and kinesics can substantially improve intelligibility, especially when it is offered in synchrony with prosodic emphasis on information being conveyed. Decades ago, David Abercrombie, a well-known British phonetician, described the relationship between prosody and non-verbal communication this way: "We speak with our vocal organs, but we converse with our whole body; conversation consists of much more than a simple interchange of spoken words" (Abercrombie, 1968, p. 55). Considerable research documents the interrelated nature of English prosody and synchronous non-verbal elements of communication (cf. Key, 1980). Contextual factors that influence a speaker's intelligibility must include the physical movements of the participants. Scholars from McNeill (1985, 1992) to Ferré (2018) have shown many ways in which prosody and gesture, including body movement, are tightly synchronized in natural oral communication. Pennycook (1985) shows the importance of this synchrony for improving the intelligibility of L2 speakers. According to Pennycook (1985):

> These 'kinesic markers' – head nods, eye blinks, small lip movements, chin thrusts, and other body movements – mark the rhythm of the speech and are produced, according to Dittman (1974), as a by-product of the speaker's ongoing task of casting thoughts into speech. Thus, such body movements provide important clues to the listener in the ongoing task of understanding what the speaker has said. (p. 263)

McNeill (1985, 1992) demonstrated early on that, for NSs of English, gesture and prosody (including pitch change, syllable length, and stress) are very tightly synchronized when they speak in oral interaction. Many subsequent studies of other languages have also shown very high integration of gesture and oral language in communicating meaning. For example, Ferré (2019) demonstrates that French speakers' hand gestures have an impact on listeners' perception of prosodic emphasis. Indeed, both gesture type (beats vs. pointing hand gestures) and gesture amplitude (large hand gestures as opposed to medium-sized or small ones) influenced prosodic highlighting in spoken French.

In studying the speech of L2 learners of English, Hardison (2016) found that their oral intelligibility was improved by the effective use of such L2 prosodic features as intonation, prominence, pausing, and rhythm, produced in synchrony with body language, or such non-verbal elements as gesture, eye contact and head movement, and body movement. Particularly important were nuclear-accented syllables in intonation phrases when they co-occurred with auditory-visual components such as fundamental frequency (F0: an acoustic cue to pitch perception), as well as hand gesture, brow raise, and head position.

Pragmatics

Yates (2017) has made a particularly strong case that pronunciation plays a vital role in performing pragmatic aspects of a language that make a speaker intelligible to any given audience. Recall that delivery coordinates:

1) a speaker's pronunciation, including segments in connected speech, word and utterance stress focused on meaning, intonation, and pitch/key;
2) non-verbals (gaze, gesture, stance, proxemics); and
3) culturally attuned use of pragmatics (especially softeners and directness in performance of speech acts).

Yates uses Bardovi-Harlig's (2013) definition of IL pragmatics as "the study of how-to-say-what-to-whom-when" (p. 68) in comparing the performance and interpretation of NSs and L2 learners of various speech acts such as requests, refusals, and compliments. That work has led to the study of interpersonal elements such as softeners, directness, and modesty-markers that "contribute to perceptions of politeness across cultures" (Yates, 2017, p. 230); such perceptions usually depend on delivery: the way such polite requests as *Can you...* are delivered. She cites Dahm and Yates' (2013) study of an Australian-based NNS doctor, Fara, and her performance in a role-played medical scenario. A surgeon viewing a video of her role-play initially had a very negative impression of Fara's performance, citing what he called her "aggressive pronunciation." After viewing her video a second time, he conceded that in spite of her pronunciation, she was doing a good and safe job. But initial impressions are important; what was it that made Fara's pronunciation sound aggressive? The researchers analyzed Fara's speech and found that, in addition to problems with unaspirated consonants, she had difficulty with intonation, not using it to emphasize stress and thought groups, so that her delivery seemed choppy. Her use of a low pitch accent in her greeting *How are you?* seemed to signal a request for "extrapropositional information" (Wennerstrom, 2001, p. 33). In other words, the lack of a high pitch nuclear accent in the greeting did not contribute to the information structure of the discourse. Other aspects of her stance and body language, such as her physical positioning relative to the patient, seemed to have made her performance seem more forceful than she intended. Yates provides a detailed curriculum for combined pronunciation and pragmatics instruction using practice-relevant models, awareness-raising activities showing interaction between pragmatics and pronunciation, and opportunities for learners to experiment with these, with feedback and further reflection. Derwing, Waugh and Munro (2021) provide empirical evidence that this kind of instruction in pragmatics does indeed improve immigrants' comprehensibility with their fellow workers in the workplace.

Because intelligibility is so closely tied to the interactional context of speaking, a holistic top-down perspective that considers interaction in social context is essential to learning and teaching intelligibility in L2 speaking (Derwing & Munro, 2015; Murphy, 2014). As we have seen, this kind of top-down orientation to IL phonology, combined with instruction on pragmatics (Yates 2017, 2021) and non-verbals (Hardison, 2016), is compatible with very recent SLA theory and research (e.g., Douglas Fir Group, 2016) which highlights the central influence of social factors on SLA and suggests a more top-down, holistic research agenda and pedagogy to further develop IL systems, including their use for purposes of intelligibility. This orientation acknowledges the central influence on L2 pronunciation of social context and interlocutors focused on negotiation of meaning – as well as the importance of pronunciation in synchrony with pragmatics and non-verbal factors such as proxemics, gesture, and facial expression – all combining to improve L2 learners' and bilinguals' intelligibility in getting their message across in social interactions. And, as we have seen, according to Yates (2017), L2 learners' delivery plays a vital role, not just in improving intelligibility, but in giving speakers better skills in "impression management": the speaker's presentation of their desired identity in interaction. As she points out, L2 learners' ability to create the impression they intend is central to their professional success (Yates, 2017, p. 228).

Accent Expressing Identity as Speaking Goal

In addition to intelligibility, a top-down approach aims for an accent that expresses an identity and cultural allegiance that the learner is comfortable with. As Yates (2017) states:

> Accent and pragmatic behaviour and values are crucial to our identity, our sense of who we are and who we align with. Thus the acquisition of a second accent is much more than simply identification with a sense of self and group affiliation (Lybeck, 2002; Marx, 2002; Gatbonton, Trofimovich, & Magid, 2005). ... As LeVelle [and] Levis (2014) argue, the motivation to invest in pronunciation is closely related to the desire to interact and align with a cultural group. (p. 233)

As we have seen, a top-down orientation to IL phonology espouses the view that IL forms and systems (including, and perhaps especially, phonology) are uniquely tied to the surrounding social context and to expressions of speaker identity. We have noted Major's (2001) statement that asking an L2 learner to adopt TL phonemes and prosodic patterns is asking them to redefine themselves as having a new identity or personality, or to come across as persons allied with a particular group's cultural values. Considerable research has established the important role played by pronunciation in social communications of identity, group membership, and cultural allegiance.

As early as the 1960's and 1970's, Alexander Guiora proposed that speakers have a "language ego" (an expression of identity) that is closely tied to IL phonology and pronunciation. Based on Taylor, Guiora, Catford, and Lane's (1969) previous research findings showing significant correlations between measures of empathy and "pronunciation proficiency" – a construct tied to the then-accepted target of NS accent – Guiora et al. (1972) argued that L2 pronunciation is profoundly influenced by a learner's empathy with speakers of the L2. Increased empathy, they maintained, enables "a temporary fusion of self-object boundaries" (Guiora et al., 1972, p. 421), thereby resulting in more native-like pronunciation. To demonstrate support for this claim, Guiora et al. carried out an experiment in which native English-speaking participants ingested increased amounts of alcohol, which the authors hypothesized would promote empathy, and were then evaluated on their pronunciation of target Thai tones, vowel length, aspiration, and an initial velar nasal phoneme by blind raters who were NSs of Thai. There was no intervening variable of structuralist instruction. Correlations between alcohol levels and ratings of native-like pronunciation were significant and suggested that small amounts of alcohol could improve the ability "to authentically pronounce a second language" (Guiora et al., 1972, p. 426). Guiora et al. explained these results by arguing that as the experimental groups became more and more empathetic due to increasing small amounts of alcohol, they were increasingly willing to merge their language ego boundaries with those of the (imagined) Thai speakers they aspired to affiliate with. Unfortunately, the Guiora et al. study ultimately became more known for its innovative use of alcohol than for its underlying explanatory theory – a theory that, though it did not influence the structuralist heyday, today seems surprisingly congruent with a current top-down theoretical conceptualization of the social and contextual forces shaping SLA.

Identity and IL Phonology

Since Guiora's early work, a top-down perspective on pronunciation that explores the way a learner's accent may shift due to social variables has blossomed as research and scholarship have increasingly documented the impact of social context, ethnic group affiliation, and other sociopsychological factors on IL phonology (e.g., Gatbonton et al., 2005; Lybeck, 2002; Yates, 2017, 2021). In the following sections, we will explore many of these studies in more depth.

In examining the development of IL phonology as a variable linguistic system, from the perspective of accuracy or correctness or a native-like accent, Tarone (1978) focused on research efforts to identify factors that might impede the full development of "correct" IL phonology by adult L2 learners. The burning question was: why do adults almost never attain "perfect" or accurately native-like accents in their efforts to learn target languages, when children almost always seem to have little difficulty doing so? In Selinker's (1972) terms, what causes the "fossilization" of IL phonology forms? Tarone (1978) discussed three possible causes of fossilization being investigated by research: physiological, psychological, and socio-emotional. First, physiological causes might be either literal atrophy of muscles in the adult's mouth and tongue needed to pronounce new TL sounds (a popular explanation sometimes proposed by L2 learners themselves, though unsupported by research) or physical changes in the brain, such as lateralization. Lateralization refers to changes in cerebral dominance during maturation which might be responsible for ending a "critical period" for language learning in human development (Scovel, 1969). Second, psychological causes of adults' phonological fossilization would certainly include structuralist habit formation, but also might be based on factors addressed in newer theories of cognitive development. So, for instance, Krashen (1973) proposed that the onset of Piaget's stage of formal operations might cause L2 learners to stop unconsciously acquiring pronunciation patterns and start learning them by consciously analyzing them. Third, socio-emotional and affective forces in mature adults might affect their willingness to pronounce the TL "accurately," meaning the way NSs of that language do. Recall that Guiora and colleagues argued that adults have more rigid ego boundaries, or identities, than children do, and phonology more than any other aspect of language reflects speaker identity. In other words, adults prefer to pronounce the TL in a way that reflects their identity and culture as speakers of their first language.

Lybeck (2002) offers empirical evidence of this close relationship between IL phonology and learner identity and acculturation. She cited Schumann (1978), who had proposed the acculturation model, which predicted that SLA is an integral part of the process of acculturation to the C2 (the culture that uses the L2). Lybeck (2002) operationalized Schumann's construct of acculturation by using social network theory (Milroy, 1987), and she examined the impact of acculturation on L2 phonology. Specifically, she hypothesized that the success of adult English-speaking sojourners in Norway in acquiring more native-like Norwegian accents would directly correlate with those learners' acculturation into Norwegian society, as measured by specific features of their social networks. The participants she studied were nine American women who had lived in Norway between one and three years. Data were collected using interviews and audio-recordings twice, once at the beginning of the study and once six months later. Interviews with each participant established her social network, particularly her relationships with NSs of Norwegian. Clusters and individual ties consisting of relatives, coworkers, friends, neighbors, and/or fellow members of an association were identified, and sojourners made statements about the level of support these clusters and individuals provided them. In addition, a recording was made of participants' Norwegian speech, which was analyzed with a focus on phonology, particularly their pronunciation of Norwegian /r/ (whether pronounced as an alveolar trill or tap in Norwegian, or with an American glide /ɹ/). For the group, Lybeck found that participants who were members of close-knit multiplex social networks of Norwegians accommodated more closely in their use of Norwegian phonological features to the usage of their network, whereas participants whose social networks were more open and uniplex developed fewer native-like variants of these forms. Of interest was that, by the end of the six-month study, one participant who had begun the study producing very native-like Norwegian pronunciation was shown to have shifted back to a more American accent; her use of Norwegian /r/ actually decreased by 24.6% over the six months, from an impressive 88.9% at the beginning of the study to 66.3% at the end (Lybeck, 2002, p. 182). During this period, interviews established that this participant was perceiving a dramatic reduction in the amount of support she was getting from her Norwegian social network, including her Norwegian husband's family: "By the time of the second interview, she had decided that her time was better spent cultivating relationships with Americans than Norwegians. She perceived Norwegians as unfriendly and critical of American social practices" (Lybeck, 2002, p. 280). Lybeck's results show the strength of the nature of phonology in expressing the evolving social identities of learners. Indeed, her data illustrate the essential fluidity of the diachronic variation, or change of time, in IL phonology, which is not necessarily universally predictable and unidirectional, moving inexorably closer to TL norms. Rather, change in IL phonology may reflect backsliding, or movement away from TL norms, in cases where learners are exposed to negative cultural experiences leading them to distance their identity from those of members of the C2.

Gatbonton et al. (2005) report on two studies exploring the relationship between L2 learners' accent and their affiliation with their home ethnic group. The first focused on 24 Canadian Francophone learners of English, and the second on 84 Chinese learners of English at Canadian universities. Raters in both groups, when asked to rate the recorded speech of fellow English learners from their home ethnic group, significantly judged the degree of accuracy of their accents in speaking English to reflect their degree of loyalty to their home ethnic group. The researchers conclude that "[t]he more learners sound like the speakers of their target language, the less they are perceived by their peers to be loyal to their home group. This finding was robust, cutting across ethnic groups and sociopolitical contexts" (Gatbonton et al., 2005, p. 504). This study suggests that the social significance to the learner of their choice of accent in acquiring an L2 can be a strong counterweight to classroom assumptions that all L2 learners share the common goal of learning to speak the L2 with a native-like accent.

As part of identifying an accent that adequately conveys the identity and desired group membership of the L2 learner, the learner may seek a role model whose stance, identity, and delivery in speaking, including accent, provide a plausible alternative that meets their goals. Muir, Dörnyei, and Adolphs (2021) shed light on the widespread uses and the importance to learners of role modeling, as a highly influential part of psychological context for SLA. After noting the lack of previous research specifically on role models in SLA, they cite research that is somewhat related, including that of Norton and colleagues on identity, investment, and imagined communities (e.g., Pavlenko & Norton, 2007). Their study of 8,472 participants showed that 68% had found for themselves an English language role model, and that these models had been selected for overall command of English, paralinguistic features, personal attributes, and accent/variety of English. The role models they most frequently chose included famous people (mostly from the film/TV industry), their teachers, friends or classmates, and family members, but there was considerable variation in the characteristics of the role models they chose. (Muir et al. [2021] provide no information about how these participants used their role models to support their language acquisition.)

Chapter 3 in Review

In this chapter, we have described the top-down orientation to research and teaching of IL phonology, beginning with its replacement of "native accent" as the goal with the two related goals of intelligibility and a TL accent expressing a learner's identity. We provide a detailed account of research on intelligibility and accentedness of L2 learners in the workplace, first as graduate student instructors in universities and then in other workplaces around the world such as petrochemical and window companies. We reviewed the evidence this research has uncovered identifying three major factors that make up a speaker's delivery (Yates, 2017) and affect oral intelligibility: pronunciation, especially of prosodic features like intonation; non-verbal communication; and pragmatics.

Considerable research establishes the importance of prosody, the first component of delivery, particularly intonation and tone, in signaling the information conveyed in discourse in any language, thereby contributing to intelligibility. Different languages use prosody in different ways to signal meaning, but learners do not seem to be aware of this and, as a consequence, they often have considerable difficulty in mastering L2 prosodic patterns. The oral intelligibility of such learners can be substantially affected as a consequence. A credible body of research shows the way intonation functions in English to mark information structure and the difficulties that learners of English as an L2 have in mastering this intricate relationship. Non-verbal communication, the second component of delivery, when synchronized with the delivery of information, plays a crucial role in making speech understandable to listeners, as shown in research studies cited in this chapter. The third component of delivery that affects intelligibility is pragmatics, including the performance and interpretation of speech acts such as requests, refusals, and compliments. The way such speech acts are signaled greatly affects intelligibility.

The second goal of top-down pronunciation research and learning in acquiring an L2 replaces a native-like accent with a TL accent expressing a learner's identity. This chapter concludes with a detailed review of research showing that IL phonology is uniquely tied to expressions of speaker identity and desired group membership.

Chapter 3 Notes

1. The term *stance* has been used to refer to a range of phenomena in oral delivery. Here, although Yates lists it as non-verbal, she also uses it in her paper to characterize a speaker's pragmatic choice (cf. Yates, 2017, p. 239). See discussion of the term in Chapter 4 on pp. 54–55.

Chapter 4

Research on the Impact of Internalized Voices on Interlanguage Phonology

Agency in L2 Style-Shifting

As we have learned in previous chapters, changes to external social contextual variables such as task, setting, topic, and interlocutor have been shown to result in documented variation in IL systems, perhaps especially in phonology. One explanation for such changes is the amount of attention paid to linguistic form as a result of those external modifications (cf. Labov, 1970; Tarone, 1979). However, some mainstream sociolinguists were quick to point out that attention (a cognitive process) cannot be viewed as the root cause of a speaker's style-shifting, or variable output. Both Beebe (1982) and Bell (1984) argue that attention cannot be considered explanatory, or the root cause, but rather must be intermediary because there is always something in the social context that causes the speaker's attention to shift. For Bell, the most basic explanatory factor resulting in a shift of attention in the context of speaking has to be the audience; he coined the term *audience design* in the field of sociolinguistics to refer to the speaker's agentive process of tailoring their message(s) to a particular audience, interlocutor, or overhearer. Providing an example in the field of SLA, Rampton (1995) described the deliberate style-shifting by Pakistani youth in an ESL class in London who would produce an informal, stigmatized *me no* + [verb] variant of negation when addressing their teacher in class in lieu of the more formal and contextually appropriate variant *I don't* + [verb] – which they demonstrably knew and used elsewhere. Rampton pointed out that the L2 learners in his study demonstrated agency in choosing where and when to focus their attention on speech, resulting in a deliberate shift to a Pakistani English form in addressing their intended audience, their ESL teacher, presumably for the purpose of "impression management" (Goffman, 1959).

This notion of tailoring messages to intended audiences had been applied very early on to studies describing style-shifting in L2 pronunciation. In two related studies referred to briefly in Chapter 2, Beebe (1977, 1981) demonstrated how an interlocutor's ethnicity systematically influenced the phonological variants produced by speakers. In these studies, both adult and child Chinese-Thai bilinguals living in Thailand conversed in Thai with either an ethnically Thai or Chinese interlocutor, producing either Thai or Chinese variants of vowels. In research by Beebe (1977), nine bilingual teachers style-shifted their pronunciation to use more Thai phonological variants when speaking Thai with ethnically Thai interlocutors and shifted to more Chinese phonological variants when speaking Thai with ethnically Chinese interlocutors. In other work by Beebe (1981), 61 Chinese-Thai bilingual fourth-graders speaking Thai used a higher percentage of Thai vowel variants when speaking with ethnically Thai interviewers, and a higher percentage of Chinese vowel variants when speaking with ethnically Chinese interviewers. Similarly, Flege (1987) published findings regarding bilinguals' phonological style-shifting in response to an interlocutor's ethnic identity; he found that French-English bilingual Canadians pronounced the phoneme /t/ differently depending on whether their interlocutor was French Canadian or English Canadian. When speaking their L2 (and also their L1) with either ethnically French or ethnically Anglo interlocutors, their phoneme /t/ was more French (i.e., more dental and unaspirated) when they were speaking to the French interlocutor, and more English (i.e., more alveolar and aspirated) when they were speaking to the Anglo interlocutor.

What is it about interlocutor identity that leads speakers to style-shift and thus modify their own pronunciation patterns in this way? Beebe and Giles' (1984) Speech Accommodation Theory (SAT), now called Communication Accommodation Theory (CAT; cf. Giles, 2016), posits that speakers adapt their speech patterns to accommodate to those of interlocutors with whom they want to identify, while diverging from those of interlocutors for whom they feel little affinity. This bidirectional accommodation can occur at the micro level in interpersonal interactions, as described in the aforementioned studies, but it can also be very prevalent at the macro level, shaping group members' pronunciation and speech patterns based on cultural group affiliation, dominant social discourses, and overarching beliefs and ideologies at play. Both Lybeck (2002, reviewed in Chapter 3) and Marx (2002), for example, report on changing pronunciation and speech patterns over time as a result of cultural group affiliation. Marx describes how she – a proud Canadian living in Germany – initially appropriated a French accent instead of an Anglo accent when speaking German because her greatest fear was to be mistaken for an American. She writes that her pronunciation goal was not to acquire a perfect German accent but rather to "cloak the fact [she] was a native speaker of English" (Marx, 2002, p. 272), clearly pointing to ideologies of what it means to be perceived as being American in Europe. And whereas such shifts in IL phonology may happen unconsciously, CAT credits a speaker's agency in consciously choosing either to accommodate to a dominant group's pronunciation or to a minority group's pronunciation as an expression of affinity for one or the other group (Giles, 2016, p. 4). In other words, speakers can unconsciously or consciously signal or manage interlocutors' impressions of their identities in their adoption of a given group's phonological patterns.

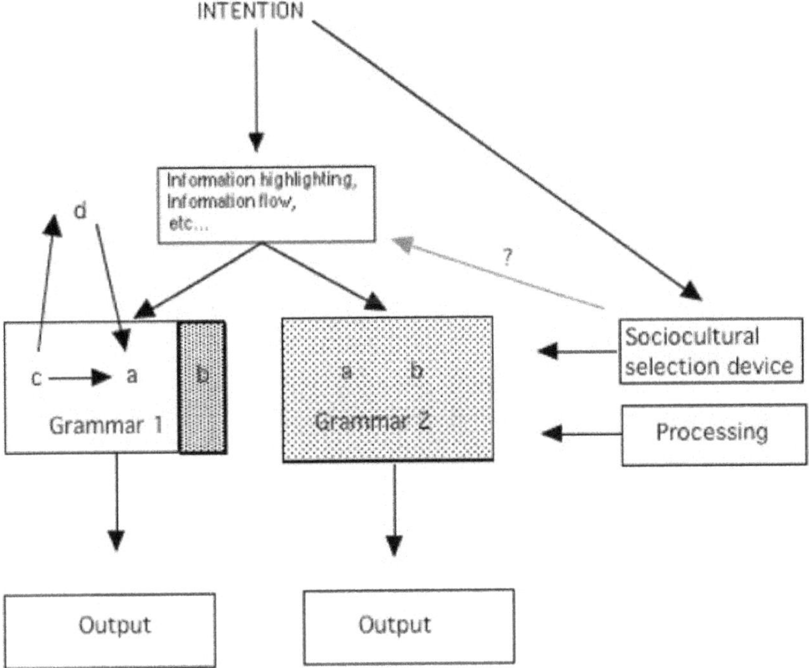

FIGURE 4.1. An Elaborated Level III Psycholinguistic Model
(Figure 3.9, Fasold & Preston, 2007, p. 66. Reproduced with permission of Cambridge University Press through PLSclear, from Fasold, Ralph, & Preston, Dennis R., *Sociolinguistic Variation Theories, Methods, and Applications.* Cambridge University Press. ©2007. All rights reserved.)

The important role of a speaker's agency is recognized in Fasold and Preston's (2007) psycholinguistic model of the bilingual brain shown in Figure 4.1 above. Based on variationist research on L2 learners, this model places speaker intention, entailing agency, at the very center, at the initiation of speaking, in its representation of how bilinguals shift their speech patterns in oral interactions with different interlocutors and audiences. Speaker intention activates a sociocultural selection device to choose between linguistic systems, accents, or other internalized tools, as well as to highlight information or manage information flow in relation to the external social contextual variables (e.g., interlocutor) previously described.

In portraying the psycholinguistics of a bilingual or bidialectal person, Figure 4.1 shows two grammars (including phonology) in boxes: one that is partially shaded (Grammar 1) and one that is fully shaded (Grammar 2). A lack of shading (as depicted in Grammar 1) represents the earliest acquired language variety, which is the variety that is the speaker's strongest; shading indicates language varieties which, because they are acquired later, are weaker than the first-acquired variety. A stronger variety is more automatic and easier to access, while a weaker variety requires more effort. In Figure 4.1, Grammar 1 – the NL of the speaker – is represented by a box that is mostly unshaded, but also has a small shaded part, because in this speaker's native grammar there are two language varieties: one is an informal variety acquired earlier at home, and the second a formal variety acquired later (perhaps in schooling or other formal instruction). The entirely shaded box, Grammar 2, represents the grammar of the IL, which is weaker overall than the speaker's NL grammar. Like Grammar 1, Grammar 2 has within it forms which vary in different linguistic and social contexts. The shading system tells us that this speaker knows two languages and that the IL is weaker overall than the NL; it also tells us that this speaker knows two dialects of their NL, and that the home dialect of their NL is stronger than the formal dialect of their NL.

The bilingual speaker's intention to use either Grammar 1 or Grammar 2, or either dialect *a* or *b*, is represented in Figure 4.1 by a sociocultural selection device that mediates between the social context of speaking and the language variety selected. So, for example, which language variety should be used given the interlocutors and social situation? Within each grammar, that same sociocultural selection device, based on sociocultural factors, mediates the speaker's choice of variants in an inherently variable linguistic construction (e.g., *a* or *b* in Grammar 2). To exemplify, Fasold and Preston cite Marsh's (1981) study of doctor-patient interaction, where a bidialectal doctor's use of either the definite article (from their later-acquired, more formal dialect *b*) or the pronominal (in their first-acquired, more informal dialect *a*) in sentences like *How's the pain in the/your hand?* depends on their assessment of sociocultural facts of power, solidarity, and familiarity entailed in the social status of the patient and length of their relationship. According to Marsh, a more formal and distant relationship between a doctor and patient would lead to use of the definite article *the* as opposed to the more informal and familiar pronominal *your*. As Fasold and Preston say, this social contextual information is paramount in choosing the linguistic elements that communicate a speaker's intention:

> After you know what you want to say and have "contextualized" it according to information status (including knowledge of your interlocutor's information state, causing the hedge between the *information* and *sociocultural* components), you go to your *grammar* to choose those things that reveal your intention (and information organization). (Fasold & Preston, 2007, p. 48)

In addition to showing how social context can influence selection of a particular language or linguistic construction or accent, Figure 4.1 also shows how one linguistic factor can influence selection of another. Two examples are drawn from Nadasdi's (1995) study of subject-doubling in Ontario French:

EXAMPLE 4.1. Subject Noun Phrase Doubling in Ontario French

Mes parents ɪʟs *étaient partis.*   *Le gars* ɪʟ *a lâché l'école.*
(My parents ᴛʜᴇʏ left.)   (The guy ʜᴇ dropped out of school.)
                                        (Nadasdi, 1995, pp. 5 & 8)

Such subject-doubling (perhaps falling into category *a* in Grammar 1, in reference to Fasold and Preston's model) is more likely to occur when the subject is specific (i.e., the referent is easily identifiable, like in the example with *Mes parents*, "My parents") and when the subject is an agent of a transitive verb like *lâcher*. If we were to rewrite Nadasdi's examples to include both a highly specific subject and a transitive verb, we might have a construction such as *Mon père* ɪʟ *a lâché l'école* ("My father ʜᴇ dropped out of school"). Co-occurring linguistic features such as these (i.e., subject specificity and a transitive verb) – indicated by *c* in Grammar 1 in Figure 4.1 – favor subject-doubling in Ontario French and thus exert an influence (depicted as an arrow in the figure) on using informal variant *a* (i.e., subject-doubling) over formal variant *b* (i.e., a subject consisting of a single noun phrase) in Grammar 1. Subject-doubling can also be favored by a sociocultural factor (*d* in Grammar 1) such as the degree of specificity in the information structure of the discourse, as when (perhaps) the speaker wants special focus on *mon père* in contrast to someone else.

Fasold and Preston's (2007) model of the psycholinguistics of a bilingual/bidialectal person provides very useful background for the ensuing discussion of sociocultural theory in SLA.

Sociocultural Theory

As depicted in Fasold and Preston's (2007) model of the psycholinguistics of a bilingual/bidialectal person, there is a relationship between sociocultural factors – variables such as interlocutor, audience, and task – and linguistic variation, but what exactly are the psychological dynamics of that relationship? Vygotsky's (1978) Sociocultural Theory (SCT) of psychological processes, although it does not have much to say about the sociolinguistic variables of audience, interlocutor identity, and impression management as represented by Fasold and Preston (2007), does help us to understand in more detail the dynamics of how sociolinguistic variation relates to cognition. It does so in its description of the developmental potential that exists between individuals and "tools/artifacts" that can be used, mastered, and (re)appropriated over time for use in new contexts and for new purposes, potentially beyond the original scope of the tool. SCT posits that all higher order cognitive functions, including language, develop by a process of mediation and through interaction with our social environments (Lantolf, 2000, 2006; Lantolf, Thorne, & Poehner, 2015). According to SCT, language exists first in the social environment and is acquired through a sociocognitive process of internalization – "the process through which individuals appropriate social forms of mediation, including cultural artifacts such as language, and use it to regulate their own mental activity" (Lantolf & Beckett, 2009, p. 460). By means of interaction with the external social environment and the linguistic forms found there, language becomes internalized and accessible for use in different interactions through a sociocultural selection device, as represented in Fasold and Preston's (2007) model of the psycholinguistics of the bilingual, as an internalized cognitive resource or tool (Lantolf et al., 2015; Vygotsky, 1981).

Consider, for example, one of the many L2 learners surveyed in Muir et al.'s (2021) study on L2 learners' use of role models in language learning, reviewed in Chapter 3. At some point in their L2 acquisition process, for whatever reason, students may attempt to sound more like their role models. For example, Marx (2002) wanted to speak German with a French accent to avoid being identified as American. Relying on video or audio-recordings of their role models, for instance, they might practice imitating individuals whom they want to emulate, rehearsing parts of a dialogue or perhaps a well-known or otherwise impactful speech to sound and even move like their role model. This could be in order to position themselves as a member of a group or as possessing an attribute or set of attributes which the role model represents (e.g., to sound more trustworthy or more professional), to tell a joke or story from that person's perspective, or to otherwise manage the impression their audience has of them. Vygotsky's concept of internalization argues that as students internalize these behaviors (i.e., as they speak with the voices of their role models, modifying their speech patterns to sound more like their role models and even to move the way they do), they require the external support of whatever video or audio-recordings they previously relied on less and less until, eventually, they no longer need it because their cognition and even their identity have been transformed by the internalization of these behaviors.

In a study exploring the developmental potential of L2 curriculum materials for learners' pronunciation development, LaScotte (2022) documents how student-selected video-recorded materials and their transcripts acted as tools to improve correlates of intelligibility for seven ESL learners studying in an intensive English language program. He argues that as students rehearsed with these tools over the course of seven weeks, different aspects of their chosen models' speech patterns were internalized; in this way, use of these student-selected materials resulted in a more individualized and differentiated vehicle for L2 pronunciation instruction for students who came from a range of NL backgrounds and thus had different pronunciation needs.

Of course, it is not uncommon for language learners to find themselves exposed to language outside of L2 curriculum materials – e.g., at home, at school, at work, at religious services, or at other typical locations for social gatherings – and in interaction with different speakers of, and possible role models for, (distinct) language varieties – regional or dialectal variations or other varieties based on age, gender identity, race, class, or level of educational attainment. There is an obvious potential for one to select a wide range of role models and internalize myriad linguistic forms and features from our many surrounding environments. SCT, its role visualized in Fasold and Preston's (2007) model of the bilingual brain, helps us to understand the dynamics of how these different language varieties can come to co-exist in the mind of the L2 learner and become so much a part of their IL system that they can later be used in new social contexts and for new purposes.

Internalizing Voices

In discussing SCT, it is imperative not to dismiss the importance of social context and social variables in the process of internalization. We maintain that when we appropriate language from our social environments, these words, phrases, and other linguistic features are not internalized in their raw forms, divorced from social context, but as sets of personalized "voices" – complexes of linguistic and non-linguistic features that embody a particular speaker's emotion, personal stance, and group identification (Tarone, 2019; Wertsch, 1991, 2002). In the early twentieth century, Bakhtin, a Russian literary theorist and contemporary of Vygotsky, theorized that centralizing forces pull in the language that surrounds us in everyday social contexts into what he termed *dialogized heteroglossia* or the coexistence of many distinctive language varieties in an authentic environment "in which [these varieties] live and take shape" (Bakhtin, 1934/1981, p. 272). At its conception, this theory originally applied to literary analysis of the contemporary novel and to literary authors who drew upon others' voices in their own works. However, this theory has since grown to include other areas of scholarship pertaining to language, including SLA, discourse analysis, and language education.

According to Bakhtin's (1934/1981) theory of dialogized heteroglossia and multivoicedness, our voice is not univocal; it incorporates voices previously encountered in surrounding social context(s). Bakhtin further theorizes that these voices cannot be divorced from social context in that the very life of a word is carried "from one mouth to another, from one context to another context, from one social collective to another, from one generation to another generation" (Bakhtin, 1963/1984, p. 202). Wertsch (1991), in his own words as cited below, underscores this point and calls attention to the importance of the sociocultural construct of voice in providing a coherent account of the human mind:

> ... [F]or Bakhtin the notion of voice cannot be reduced to an account of vocal-auditory signals. Although he was often interested in the concrete

qualities of voice quality,[1] his account of the speaking consciousness is more general. It applies to written as well as spoken communication, and it is concerned with the broader issues of a speaking subject's perspective, conceptual horizon, intention, and world view. Throughout his analysis Bakhtin stressed the idea that voices always exist in a social milieu; there is no such thing as a voice that exists in total isolation from other voices. (Wertsch, 1991, pp. 51–52)

Hastings and Manning (2004), building on Wertsch, describe Bakhtin's constructs of heteroglossia and voice in this way:

Repertoires... are assembled out of a social heteroglossia that consists of a number of distinct "voices" of others that have been appropriated into a single speaker's repertoire or into the "dialogized heteroglossia" of a system of stylistic registers. The anchoring points of a stylistic continuum along which speakers position themselves sociocentrically with respect to their conversational partners are often the voices of exemplary others; stereotyped, essentialized voices of exemplary others are crucial to anchoring the linguistic system by which speakers index their own situational and social positions. (Hastings & Manning, 2004, pp. 300–301)

According to Hastings and Manning, there's a dialogue between the individual's identity (the "self") and what they call the "alterity:" the identities of those exemplary others who influence "the acts of speakers expressing or voicing some self" (Hastings & Manning, 2004, p. 291). In other words, individuals not only internalize and store language as sets of linguistic forms (e.g., pitch contours, stress patterns, words, phrases, and collocations); they store voices which characterize their original speakers and retain aspects of the original speaker's particular emotion, social identity, and ideology within a particular community – one of many in a larger society.

Lantolf and Thorne (2006) discuss a memorable example showing how voices are internalized through a process of mediation and can later be drawn upon as psychological/cultural tools (cf. Lantolf & Thorne, 2006, pp. 138–142). In Eva Hoffman's (1989) autobiography *Lost in Translation*, she writes about her transition from "Ewa" (her original, Polish name) to "Eva" (her Anglicized name). During this period in her life, she sought out Anglo voices to fill the loss of her inner Polish voice. She writes:

Since I lack a voice of my own, the voices of others invade me as if I were a silent ventriloquist. They ricochet within me, carrying on conversations, lending me their modulations, intonations, and rhythms. I do not yet possess them; they possess me. But some of them satisfy a need; some of them stick to my ribs. I could take on that stylish, ironic elongation which is X's mark of perpetual amusement; it fits something in my temperament, I could learn to speak a part of myself through it. And that curtailed, deliberate dryness that Y uses as an antidote to sentiment opens a door into a certain New England sensibility whose richness I would never otherwise understand. Eventually, these voices enter me; by assuming them, I gradually make them mine. (Hoffman, 1989, p. 220)

Some of these voices appealed to her, and others did not; Hoffman internalized and reappropriated those that suited her – to make them her own – and left the ones that did not. In this way, these Anglo voices served Hoffman as tools for her new way of thinking as she constructed her identity as an Anglo academic woman (Lantolf, personal communication to LaScotte, June 4, 2021). Therefore, speaking with a certain voice can index the speaker as a member of a particular social group (Blackledge & Creese, 2014), position the speaker in a certain role, e.g., the hero, the victim, or the joke-teller (Wortham, 2001), or otherwise lead the audience to have a desired impression of the speaker (Goffman, 1959; Yates, 2017). This indexicality and positioning can be further seen in a speaker's stylization or use of "double voicing."

Voice and Language Play in SLA

Bakhtin defines double voicing as "an artistic representation of another's linguistic style, an artistic image of another's language" (Bakhtin, 1934/1981, p. 362). In this type of stylization, there are (at least) two voices present in the moment of speaking or writing: the voice of the person who is stylizing and the voice of the person(s) whose style is being represented. In this way, the use of others' voices and a person's stylization of said voices can communicate the stylizer's stance regarding both the voice and the information being conveyed (e.g., supportive or dubious, straightforward or sarcastic). Stylization can therefore allow speakers and writers to align or distance themselves from the particular voices, discourses, social groups, and ways of being (Blackledge & Creese, 2014) that they are speaking or writing about.

Bakhtin's interest in stylization and stance as conveyed in speech has been taken up, at least in part, by variationist sociolinguists such as Bell (1984), Eckert and Rickford (2001), and Kiesling (2005, 2009, 2019). For Kiesling, the term *stance* communicates who speakers are in terms of emotion, role, and ethnicity, and how stance is communicated via verbal and non-verbal means, such as when a speaker performs Australian ethnicity by using word-final *-er* or a high rising tone (cf. Kiesling, 2005). Stance also communicates a speaker's evolving relationships with both content and interlocutors during an interaction – for example, how certain they are of their statements, or how friendly or dominating they are towards their interlocutors (Kiesling, 2019).

Language play – when a speaker or writer manipulates elements of their language(s) for sarcasm, irony, or their own personal amusement – is one way in which stylizers convey stance by exploiting an interplay among multiple voices, as in double voicing. According to Bakhtin (1934/1981), stylization through double voicing allows for one to draw upon a multiplicity of voices from their heteroglossic language repertoire and, by doing so, experience a sort of linguistic liberation: "The creating consciousness stands, as it were, on the boundary line between languages and styles.... Only polyglossia fully frees consciousness from the tyranny of its own language and its own myth of language" (pp. 60–61). In language play, speakers and writers can exert agency in assuming the identities of others, reappropriating others' voices for their own purposes. This requires a certain heteroglossic use of many different voices and varieties of language, which would no doubt be of interest to teachers of L2 learners and to researchers studying SLA.

What do we know about how L2 learners perform these kinds of heteroglossic voices? While the study of language play has long remained in the periphery of SLA research, several scholars have explored L2 learners' and bilinguals' use of stylization and double voicing in language play (e.g., Belz, 2002; Broner & Tarone, 2001; R. Forman, 2011). In their account of a fifth-grade Spanish immersion classroom, for example, Broner and Tarone (2001) show how bilingual children "took on different roles and spoke with different voices, both in English and Spanish... Sometimes the children acted out parts in a drama, taking the part of someone else: a villain, a radio announcer, a rock star" (p. 372). A few focal students from Broner and Tarone's study (Leonard, in particular) illustrate double voicing nicely. In Example 4.2, Leonard stylizes his speech to speak with the voice of a villain, laughing in a stereotypically villainous way, as he repeats the teacher's announcement that there will be no recess that day:

EXAMPLE 4.2. Leonard as Villain

   1 Teacher: *no hay recreo.* (There's no recess.)
   2 Leonard: *no hay recreo.* (There's no recess.)

    3 Girl: *no hay recreo ahora.* (There's no recess now.)
    4 Leonard: *ahora? . . . ahora no hay recreo heh, heh, heh.*
                      (Now? . . . now there's no Recess heh, heh, heh)
                      (villainous voice)
                          (Example 8, Broner & Tarone, 2001, p. 372)

As in the previous example, Example 4.3 below also demonstrates the speaker's modulation of voice quality, speaking the Spanish phrase *yo no* (not me) three times, parodying other speakers by using different pitches, stress patterns, and even a foreign accent. In the first line, Leonard's pronunciation of the Spanish words *yo no* is stylized with a normal pitch level and an Anglo pronunciation pattern (foreign accent), in the second line it is stylized with an overall higher pitch level (childish), and in the third line again with normal pitch and Anglo accent and adding the proclamation *yo tengo alambre* (I have a wire) in an "authoritative voice" – heavily stressed, projecting self-importance.

EXAMPLE 4.3. Playing with Pitch Patterns

    1 Leonard: */you: nou:/, dijo Leonard.* ("not me" said Leonard)
    2   *yo no,* (high pitched voice) *dijo Leonard* (regular pitch)
                      ("not me" said Leonard)
    3   */you: nou:/ . . . yo tengo alambre:* (in authoritative voice)
                      (not me . . . I have a wire)
                          (Example 11, Broner & Tarone, 2001, p. 373)

And, finally, in Example 4.4 below, we see Leonard using double voicing to parody the voice of his classmate, Brandon, sarcastically. Leonard describes and re-enacts what happened earlier that day during computer time when he had been bothering another student (Brandon), who then made an obscene gesture at Leonard.

EXAMPLE 4.4. Leonard as "Brandon"

    1 Leonard: *Este² es que Brandon hizo.* [obscene gesture]
                      (This is what Brandon did).
    2 Carolina: *Él estaba en el computador hicí 'mira como este'* and and and
                      (He was on the computer, he did "look at this" and and and)
    3 Marvin: *Sí. un montículo.* (Yes. A mound.)
    4 Leonard: I was like 'Brandon?' and he's *'no es mi culpa que uso mi dedo
                      medio para mí'*
                      (it's not my fault I use my middle finger for myself)
                          (Example 9, Broner & Tarone, 2001, p. 372)

In each of these examples, but especially in the latter (Example 4.4), it is important to recognize that Brandon is not parroting his teacher, himself, or a fellow student exactly in the way their utterances were previously said. Simply put, Leonard is not a tape-recorder. Rather, Leonard stylizes his speech with the use of double voicing to produce sarcasm: "the sort of parody that Bakhtin (1934/1981) discusses at length, in which one speaks with the voice of another while maintaining his or her own voice as commentary" (Broner & Tarone, 2001, p. 372).

Since Broner and Tarone's (2001) study, an increasing number of scholars have documented the occurrence of language play and double voicing in multilingual speech. Vang's (2013) analysis of Japanese-English bilinguals, for instance, found that participants drew on their linguistic repertoires in both Japanese and English, code-switching between the two languages to mark changes in the speaker's role or voice. For example, participants in the study would perform the voice of other Japanese individuals in Japanese, even though the rest of the conversation would be mostly in English. Vang theorized that switching to Japanese in these instances further dramatized the narratives, which is reminiscent of Wertsch's (2002, p. 46) claim that this kind of direct re-enactment of another's words is not just "remembering" – it is "re-experiencing."

Students' use of language play and dramatization, as shown in Broner and Tarone (2001) and in Vang (2013), often makes use of what some discourse analysts have referred to as "constructed dialogue" – a creative performance of (possibly imagined or fictitious) dialogue, often marked by shifts in pronunciation and non-verbals, highlighting elements of emotion, irony, or even mockery for the narrator's own purposes (Tannen, 1989). Such instances of constructed dialogue produced by L1 speakers are often prefaced by quotatives such as, *and I go...* or *and she was like...* (Clark & Gerrig, 1990; Yule, 1993) or even by use of the "zero quotative," which is the marked absence of any word or phrase used to introduce the quoted segment (Mathis & Yule, 1994). Example 4.5 below showcases an English NS's use of constructed dialogue in oral interaction; the first is preceded by *I'm like* and the second by the zero quotative (Ø):

EXAMPLE 4.5. Types of Quotatives

1	Maya:	. . . I'm like, 'LOOK don't you'
2		(falsetto) Ø: 'No no no – I don't mean it – I don't mean it'
		(Example 8, Mathis & Yule, 1994, p. 68)

As shown in Example 4.5, constructed dialogue with zero quotatives can be – and often is (cf. Laver, 1980) – marked by a change in voice quality to dramatize a shift in speaker roles. This is what happens in Example 4.5 when Maya (the speaker) begins to speak with the voice of her "on-again-off-again" friend Ellen, shifting her pitch patterns to include a higher pitch (i.e., falsetto voice, also used by Leonard in Example 4.3) to distinguish the two characters in her constructed dialogue and perhaps to characterize Ellen as being childlike or scared to upset Maya. In this sense, constructed dialogue and the dramatized effect achieved by the use of quotatives (including the zero quotative) marked with changes in voice quality fit well with the Bakhtinian construct of voice in SCT.

Continuing this line of research on double voicing and constructed dialogue in L2 speech, recent scholarship has begun to explore the interface between the SCT constructs of voice and double voicing, and IL competence – the linguistic system hypothesized to underlie learner language. Taking a transdisciplinary stance to bridge sociocultural, sociolinguistic, and psycholinguistic (i.e., cognitive) dimensions, LaScotte (2016, 2019) explores how the voices that L2 learners have previously internalized are later drawn upon in re-creation for delivery in unrehearsed oral narratives; these voices are analyzed using a multidimensional model measuring syntactic complexity, accuracy, and fluency[3] (CAF), which are shown to vary systematically from one voice to another. In the study, LaScotte recorded narratives produced by two French-English bilinguals, Sylvie and Marine, who were first-year teachers of French at an immersion school. In these narratives, two types of voices were identified and compared in terms of CAF: (1) each speaker's baseline narrative voice and (2) the voices of various characters they portrayed through use of vocal stylization and double voicing in constructed dialogue. Upon comparing these voices for both Sylvie and Marine, clear differences were found, especially in terms of the speakers' grammatical accuracy and fluency in English. When these speakers enacted the voice of someone more proficient than they were in English (e.g., an English-speaking student or one of the students' parents), that voice became more accurate in terms of the English syntax and morphology and more fluent than the speaker's baseline narrative voice.

For example, Sylvie – the less proficient speaker of the two – only marked present tense verbs for third person singular when she used double voicing to dramatically re-enact the voice of one of the student's native-English-speaking parents; in all other instances of her baseline narrative, she used the bare form of the verb. Examples 4.6 depicts this (markings for analysis-of-speech unit boundaries were removed from the originals for clarity; boldface emphasis appears in the originals).

EXAMPLE 4.6. Sylvie marks third-person singular in present tense enacted voice (in bold)

   1   But Amendine sayed me that told me that she receive a mail of a
   2   father who ask her to say to his son that the one of his toy were locked
   3   in a tree on their garden was now in her bedroom and he take the toys in
   4   the tree I don't know what ... and just he sent a mail to Amendine to
   5   say "You can say to my son that he **has** now his toy."

(Example 6, LaScotte, 2019, p. 54)

Example 4.6 demonstrates a typical error Sylvie made throughout the entire duration of data collection. Whenever she spoke in the present tense – in her narrative voice – she used the bare form of the verb, meaning she did not mark the verb for third person (*she receive a mail, he take the toys*). The sole instance of her correctly marking for the third person singular subject in the present tense appears in line 5 (*he **has** now his toy*), and it occurs when she is attributing speech to one of the school children's parents.

Just as Sylvie was able to become more grammatically accurate when enacting the voice of this child's English-speaking father, participants were able to "downshift" their English accuracy in their portrayal of speakers whom they felt were less proficient. Marine – the more proficient speaker – did this when attributing speech in constructed dialogue to her conversation partner, Sylvie. In Example 4.7, Marine interjects herself in Sylvie's narrative, attributing speech to Sylvie in a dialogue for which she was not originally present, creatively inserting herself into the story. In line 5, when Marine speaks with Sylvie's voice, she makes an error in syntax in her question *"Why did you do?"* – an error that Marine never made in her baseline narrative voice or during the many instances where she posed questions to her conversation partner. The speakers in this dialogue are Sylvie ("S") and Marine ("M").

EXAMPLE 4.7. Marine's error in syntax when enacting Sylvie's voice

   1 S: Yeah, and Lesley was here too and, so Victor, Clarice, me, and Noah. And
   2   Noah was talking with Lesley and Lesley ask her for the costume, and
   3   Noah just say "Oh yeah, we're doing all the characters of Mario" and
   4   Victor, Clarice, and me were like "Noah, it's a secret."
   5 M: **"Why did you do?"** (speaking in the voice of Sylvie)
   6 S: "Oh, I didn't know that." (speaking as Noah) How it's possible. So, yeah.

(Table 3, LaScotte, 2019, p. 55)

This study is of interest because unlike previous sociolinguistic studies discussed at length in Chapter 3 and at the beginning of this chapter (Chapter 4), the causes of variation here are not identifiable in the objective external social context, such as in terms of a speaker's physically present interlocutor, audience, or task. While Sylvie and Marine are speaking, their audience remains the same (each other), as does the task/activity (telling stories to one another). While this immediate environment stays the same, when the speakers enact others' voices in relation to internally imagined social contexts, both their grammatical accuracy and overall fluency shift (as does their lexicon, cf. LaScotte, 2019 for more examples).

Building on LaScotte (2016, 2019), LaScotte and Tarone (2019) expanded their participant base to examine whether this phenomenon occurs with other speakers from a range of proficiency levels and L1 backgrounds. Analyzing the speech produced by 10 adult L2 learners of English, and focusing primarily on fluency and grammatical features of these voices, LaScotte and Tarone (2019) found that all 10 learners produced statistically significantly more fluent (p value = 0.01757812) and grammatically accurate (p value = 0.001953125) speech when enacting the voices of imagined protagonists – who were often times more proficient or NSs of the TL – in their narratives than when speaking in their own baseline voice. These enacted voices contained significantly fewer instances of false starts, repetitions, reformulations, and replacements. Whereas the measured amount of change between voices differed by speaker, this study demonstrates that, overall, the voices that these L2 learners have internalized, shaped by the social context(s) in which they were embedded, resulted in variable linguistic patterns of fluency, grammar, and vocabulary when enacted in completely different socially contextualized narratives (e.g., story or joke-telling). Although there was no change in the social characteristics of their physical environment – that is, there was no change in terms of physically present interlocutor, task, or topic – the voices appear to have become part of the learners' competence and can be invoked at will for newly imagined social contexts and new purposes in these learners' creative narratives.

While the studies reviewed above on IL CAF did document shifts in fluency, a speaker's enactment of different voices has also been shown to specifically affect IL pronunciation patterns. For example, Rampton (2013) considered the impact of voices on a speaker's stylization in constructed dialogue in his analysis of a bilingual speaker, Mandeep, who began to use English later in life. Rampton found that Mandeep's language production more closely approximated phonological elements of different local varieties of English when he was speaking with others' voices (in comparison to his base style pronunciation).

Similarly, Moreno (2016) demonstrated how Heriberto, an adult L2 English-speaking immigrant, could invoke the voices of others that he had previously internalized for new communicative purposes. In her analysis of Heriberto's spontaneous narratives, Moreno found that Heriberto produced more target-like English pronunciation patterns when, in constructed dialogue, he enacted the voices of various Anglo people he knew (e.g., a coworker, a former roommate). Analyzing Heriberto's suprasegmental pronunciation, Moreno found that his performance of the voices of these NSs of English resulted in stylistic changes that reflected local accents of English, which contrasted with his typical Hispanic English pronunciation patterns when speaking as himself.

Take, for instance, Example 4.8 and Figure 4.2 below, which together showcase the differences between these stylistic patterns in Heriberto's recount of a single narrative. In this excerpt taken from Moreno (2016), Heriberto uses constructed dialogue to perform the voice of his roommate, Matt, a NS of English white male in his late 20s, in his recount of a conversation between the two of them. In Moreno's analysis of this example, she describes a difference in voice quality following Heriberto's use of the discourse quotative *goes like*, as he introduces Matt's voice, creating what she refers to as a "vocal flutter" in the words *bro* and *heck*, stylizing this voice to be like the voice of a "stereotypical 'surfer' or 'skater'" (Moreno, 2016, p. 25).

EXAMPLE 4.8. *"Bro, what the heck are you doin?"* (Double voicing "Matt")

1	Heriberto:	And my **ROOM**mate (.) MATT comes into the ROOM
2		and he knows obviously that I'm chatting with LEah
3		And then he goes like (.) '**BRO** (.) what the HECK are you **DO**in?'
4		And then I just told him tell I TOLD him
5		'oh I'm just goin on a date with LEah @virtual @world'
		(Example 2, Moreno, 2016, p. 24)

Heriberto begins in lines 1–2 by setting up the story (his roommate enters the room while he is speaking with Leah) and moves into constructed dialogue, with Matt's words in line 3, and his own in line 5. (Word and sentence-level stress are illustrated in this example by use of capitalization and boldface font, with words in boldface font receiving the focus stress; the @ symbol represents laughter; these transcription conventions come from Moreno [2016].) Moreno's acoustic analysis docu-ments a dramatic shift in intonation and rhythm between his portrayal of Matt's voice in line 3 and his own voice in line 5.

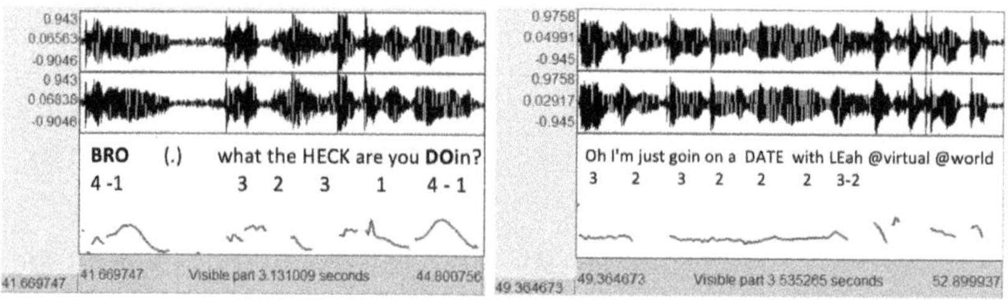

FIGURE 4.2. Praat Display, "Matt" Voice v. "Self" Voice
(Figure 1.3, Moreno, 2016, p. 25. Reproduced with permission from Moreno, Leah, *Channeling Charlie: Suprasegmental Pronunciation in a Second Language Learner's Performance of Others' Voices.* ©2016. All rights reserved.)

Figure 4.2 displays lines 3 and line 5 side by side using speech analysis software Praat[4] (Boersma & Weenink, n.d.), and applies Pike's (1945) four-level system of intonation[5]. In line 3, Heriberto is performing Matt's voice, which is characterized by rising and falling intonation contours and sentence-level stress (including focus stress or prominence) towards the stress-timed end of the continuum (Dauer, 1983) – consistent with local pronunciation patterns of English. Using Praat, we can easily observe that Heriberto uses a much wider intonation range – from level 1 to level 4 when performing Matt's voice. Compare these patterns to line 5, where we see Heriberto's performance of his own voice, with stress more evenly distributed across all syllables in the utterance and where his intonation range is much flatter – only moving from level 2 to level 3, which communicates diffidence in English and is more characteristic of his Hispanic pronunciation patterns. (Spanish occurs at the syllable-timed end of the language continuum, cf. Dauer, 1983.) As demonstrated by this and other examples (cf. Moreno, 2016), Heriberto's suprasegmentals became more English-like when enacting the voice of a native-speaker of English, and more Spanish-accented[6] when enacting his own English voice.

Chapter 4 in Review

In this chapter, we have examined the agentive process of style-shifting as speakers choose when and where to direct their attention to linguistic form, and whether or not to accommodate to and/or parody the phonological patterns of their interlocutors for purposes of impression management or language play. Not only do social contextual variables such as task and interlocutor affect a speaker's performance in the language; social factors have been argued to have an impact on a speaker's cognition, influencing their IL development and overall linguistic competence. According to SCT, the language we are exposed to in our environment(s) is internalized not in its raw form but retains elements of its original social context, constituting what several scholars have referred to as voices. Over time, these voices become accessible as a cognitive resource and can be invoked at will by the speaker for new purposes such as impression management or language play.

Several studies reviewed in this chapter have explored how multilingual learners draw upon such internalized voices for their own amusement (i.e., in language play) and in creative re-enactments and reconstructions of past narrative events, often in constructed dialogue. In this way, speakers exert agency in assuming the identities of others by means of vocal stylization (or double voicing) in their performances, positioning themselves and others in one light or another. The findings of these studies suggest that L2 learners' proficiency entails access to and use of many distinct internalized voices that can differ substantially from one another both in terms of grammatical accuracy and fluency, and of pronunciation, such as in suprasegmental elements such as intonation, rhythm, and pausing. These findings raise questions for L2 instruction, particularly: how can teachers create a space for their students to adopt and internalize a range of voices (including more target-like voices) for their own purposes? In terms of IL phonology and pronunciation instruction, such theoretical frameworks and research findings suggest the benefits of using a top-down, holistic teaching approach to the teaching of pronunciation – one that accepts the idea of a multi-voiced IL competence – by which a learner shifts pronunciation to enact different L2 voices to signal each speaker's emotion, personal stance, and identification with different speech communities, both in impression management and in creative language play.

Chapter 4 Notes

1. In Wertsch's (1991) description of "concrete qualities of voice quality," he is referring to different physical characteristics of speech such as changes to pitch range (high pitched, low pitched) and Catford's (1964) short list of examples of different phonation types; his list includes falsetto, breathy voice, creaky voice, whispery voice.

2. *Este* should be *esto*. L2 learners in immersion programs, like NL learners, make errors. There is a long history of commentary on the nature of such errors, their causes, and ways to remediate them over time, while retaining a focus on use of the L2 to learn and discuss school content.
3. Disfluent speech – speech that contains false starts, repetitions, reformulations, and/or excessive pausing – can have a significant impact on a speaker's intelligibility and the listener's ease of understanding. For this reason, we include oral fluency as part of a speaker's overall pronunciation.
4. A brief description of how to read Praat readouts is included here for the reader and uses Figure 4.2 as an example. Along the bottom of Figure 4.2, the length of the speech segment is indicated (with start and stop times of the .mp3 file) in seconds; these segments are each about three seconds long. The two rows at the top of the visual display the amplitude in a stereo wave form of the speech utterance over time, showing loudness, syllable length, and pausing. The bottom row of the visual indicates pitch contours. The text (Heriberto's utterances) was added onto the figure by Moreno (2016) and is not a feature of Praat.
5. Pike (1945) posited that there are four pitch levels in American English ranging from 4 (extra high) to 1 (low). As Celce-Murcia, Brinton, and Goodwin (2010) state, "[t]hese levels are highly dependent on discourse meaning and prominence, with rises and falls in intonation co-occurring with the highlighted, or more important, words that receive prominence within the sentence" (p. 231). Take for example the sentence "I like it" with the pitch patterns 2-3-1: this would be unmarked for any special emphasis; 2-4-1 would be 'I LIKE it' (with special emphasis placed on 'like'); and 2-3-2 would be a non-final ending as in 'I like it … [but]'.
6. By Spanish-accented here, we mean employing a more syllable-timed rhythm. We are not implying that his accent, according to Munro and Derwing (1995), has changed.

Chapter 5

Top-Down Pronunciation Pedagogies with a Focus on Voice and Intelligibility

Recommendations for Top-Down Pronunciation Instruction

As we have shown (see Chapters 2 and 3), the central goal for pronunciation teaching and learning has shifted over the past few decades. Whereas a native-like accent approximating that of an ideal NS was previously the target for many language learners and their teachers in traditional pronunciation classrooms (including general ESL education programs), a new goal of intelligibility – which is whether interlocutors can actually understand learners' pronunciation in a given social context – has gradually emerged and is presently the central aim of L2 teaching and learning. With this new focus on clear communication in a range of environments, ranging from workplace communication programs to ITA training programs, pronunciation teachers have needed to shift the focus of their teaching. Traditional, explicit instruction on phonology, for example, focused on minimal pair drills targeting students' accurate pronunciation of isolated segments and words, cannot achieve this new goal of intelligibility. This new goal is better served by a focus on supra-segmental instruction, with attention to larger, discourse-level aspects of speech such as stress, rhythm, and intonation, as well as segmentals when they occur in stressed syllables (cf. Hahn, 2004; Morley, 1991; Wong, 1987; Zielinski, 2015).

So, what types of pedagogical guidelines and teaching methods can easily lend themselves to address a wide range of issues related to intelligibility to meet all manner of learner goals while still keeping students' unique pronunciation needs at the center of instruction? Early on, Pennington and Richards (1986; see also Pennington, 1989) called for a shift from a "phonemic-based" to a "discourse-based" and meaning-focused orientation to teaching L2 pronunciation; they provided a list of general recommendations, which we reproduce here, as a beginning framework for top-down pronunciation pedagogy:

1. The teaching of pronunciation must focus on [learners'] longer term goals; short-term objectives must be developed with reference to long-term goals.
2. The goal of any explicit training in pronunciation should be to bring learners gradually from controlled, cognitively based performance to automatic, skill-based performance.
3. Teaching should aim toward gradually reducing the amount of native language influence on segmental, voice-setting, and prosodic features but should not necessarily seek to eradicate totally the influence of the native language on the speaker's pronunciation in the second language.
4. Pronunciation ought to be taught as an integral part of oral language use, as part of the means for creating both referential and interactional meaning, not merely as an aspect of the oral production of words and sentences.
5. Pronunciation forms a natural link to other aspects of language use, such as listening, vocabulary, and grammar; ways of highlighting this interdependence in teaching need to be explored.

(Pennington & Richards, 1986, p. 219)

If teachers were to interpret this list of general recommendations in order of their appearance, a focus on students' unique pronunciation goals, such as their need to communicate in specific work settings (see Chapter 2), would be of primary importance, followed by the need for moving from controlled practice with attention-raising activities to autonomous use in real-world contexts, and the recommendation to not seek to completely remove a learner's NL accent. As we saw in Chapter 2, Major (2001) underscores the importance of retaining one's NL accent; along with several other scholars reviewed in Chapters 3 and 4 (e.g., Guiora et al., 1972; Lybeck, 2002; Marx, 2002; Yates, 2017), he considers NL accent to be an expression of identity and personality. Müller (2013) concurs, positioning learner identity and autonomy as central to a top-down approach to L2 pronunciation instruction; she states, "pronunciation is intricately linked to speakers' identity negotiations in L2-mediated interactions and their relative willingness to adjust to different speech communities" (p. 216). The central importance of learner autonomy and personal engagement in the process of forming an L2 phonology is also stressed by Moyer (2017), who argues that learners create their own unique personae and identities in adopting specific L2 accents to express "possible selves" in the new culture (p. 401).

In application of several of these insights, Yates (2017, reviewed in Chapter 3) offers a more recent framework for pronunciation teaching that focuses on the pragmatics of the social situation in which learners aim to practice. The elements comprising her PREFER framework are:

P: Practice-relevant models
R: Raising awareness of pragmatic and pronunciation issues and their interaction
E: Experimentation with new pragmatic resources and pronunciation
F: Feedback
E: Exploring the world outside
R: Reflection on what to do and how to do it.

(Yates, 2017, p. 240)

Like Pennington and Richards (1986), Yates (2017) places learners' unique pronunciation goals and vocational needs at the center of instruction as she argues that "practice-relevant," authentic or semi-authentic (i.e., adapted) speech samples are crucial in order to provide students with input that accurately reflects the language used in target communities. Like Pennington and Richards, Yates suggests that students move from controlled, awareness-raising activities to experimentation, or automatic skill-based practice, in which instructors (and perhaps peers) provide students with necessary feedback for improvement, and students are then asked to apply what they have learned to new contexts and reflect on how they feel about their performance and what could possibly be improved in future interactions. And although Yates' PREFER framework *per se* does not explicitly reference either NL accent or expressions of identity, Yates does make it clear early on in her writing that "accent and pragmatic behaviour and values are crucial to our identity, our sense of who we are and who we align with" (Yates, 2017, p. 233).

Drawing upon the research we have presented so far in this book and elsewhere (see also LaScotte, Meyers, & Tarone, 2021), we suggest that curriculum materials such as textbooks, worksheets, mobile applications, audio and video files, and other instructional resources take a top-down approach to pronunciation teaching and learning by beginning with an emphasis on social context and purpose. We further suggest that these materials be adapted by the teacher and contextualized to the local pedagogical and learning context(s) in order to address students' unique social, professional, and/or academic goals. In doing so, we follow the pedagogical guidelines and teaching methods initially presented by Pennington and Richards (1986) and updated in light of recent research by Yates (2017), among others (e.g., Moyer, 2017; Müller, 2013), which we believe can easily lend themselves to addressing a wide range of issues related to intelligibility and, ultimately, expression of identity as well. In such a top-down approach, not only would students have the benefit of using authentic or adapted materials immediately relevant to their interests and area(s) of study, but also the use of such materials would be congruent with recent SLA theory and research (e.g., Douglas Fir Group, 2016), highlighting the influence of social and situational factors and emphasizing the importance of community, norm, choice, identity expression, and agency in pronunciation instruction.

Table 5.1 presents a synthesis of the teaching recommendations, frameworks, and approaches that we have found in the literature so far; we will use these in evaluating the teaching methods and materials that we describe in this chapter.

In the following sections, we describe in detail the use of contextualized and authentic or adapted materials which employ this kind of top-down approach to teaching pronunciation, including those engaging such methods as tracking and shadowing as well as role-play and other drama techniques. After we review each top-down pedagogy, we present a grid (used in Tables 5.2–5.10) in which the features of that approach are evaluated in relation to the recommendations presented in Table 5.1. We conclude by previewing the Mirroring Project (which is the focus of Chapter 6) as an effective top-down pedagogical approach for L2 pronunciation instruction, and one which not only meets all five recommendations in Table 5.1 but also adds to them. The Mirroring Project focuses squarely on students' re-enactment of self-selected voices of video-recorded speakers (including their non-verbal communication patterns) to improve intelligibility and also to express the speakers' identity, emotions, and pragmatic goals.

TABLE 5.1. Synthesized Recommendations for Top-Down Pronunciation Instruction

1. Focus on unique learner goals for intelligibility: pronunciation, pragmatics, and non-verbals.	What are learners' social, academic, and/or professional goals (such as their need to communicate in specific work settings) that require intelligibility? What are students' specific pronunciation and pragmatic challenges in meeting those goals, including the use of non-verbals such as gesture and facial expression? Students from different language backgrounds, past learning contexts, and interactional experiences can have vastly different areas of need in pronunciation improvement and so instruction should be tailored to individual students whenever possible.
2. Provide elements of choice, agency, voice, and identity in students' learning.	In pursuit of their unique goals, students should be given a degree of choice and agency in deciding which of their challenges to prioritize and which pedagogical materials to use in the process. Pronunciation and accent are inextricably tied to expressions of identity and personality, and students' choices of materials and methods should reflect the identity(ies) they would like to maintain and/or construct in the L2 as well as the particular voices they wish to internalize.
3. Emphasize communication in social context.	Social and communicative context and the influence of situational factors such as the speaker's purpose, emotion, and interlocutor/audience are central in a top-down approach to pronunciation instruction focused on intelligibility. In consideration of the longer-term goals of students further developing their L2 pronunciation for social purposes, instruction should highlight important factors of emotion, the speaker's intention, and other social and pragmatic functions of language that are important for contextualizing speech samples for an intended live audience.
4. Include noticing and awareness-raising activities, controlled practice, and feedback.	Students should begin with activities that ask them to analyze the social and communicative context of speech samples and notice how word stress, rhythm, and intonation patterns shift depending on the context of speaking. In a controlled environment (such as the classroom), students should be given the opportunity to apply these features to their own speech and receive feedback from their audience (e.g., the instructor and/or their peers) and also analyze their own speech for such features in order to notice areas needing further improvement.
5. Ask learners to apply learned material to new content, followed by reflection on their own performance.	Moving from controlled practice to more holistic, skill-based performance, students should apply what they have learned to new content (e.g., in delivering an original presentation to their target community). Following this application, students should be given the opportunity to reflect on what they have learned and how well they have met their unique goals to overcome specific challenges with pronunciation, pragmatics, and non-verbals. This can help to identify areas that require further attention.

Tracking and Shadowing Pedagogies

Although the terms *tracking* and *shadowing* have been used somewhat interchangeably in pronunciation research literature and teaching materials, they refer to two slightly different pedagogical techniques. In *tracking*, students listen to a recording and imitate what the speaker is saying with as little delay as possible. Following along with the help of a transcript or subtitles, students "track" the speech segments and try to produce them exactly as they hear them. In *shadowing*, students also listen to a recording; after a short delay, they attempt to reproduce what they heard, exactly as they heard it, but without the use of a transcript or subtitles. The only differences therefore between these two techniques appear to be the amount of time that lapses between students' listening to the original segment and their subsequent imitation, and whether or not students have access to a written text or transcript. While in tracking students imitate with as little delay as possible with the help of a visual text, in shadowing, students repeat slightly after the speaker, without a transcript, and may even pause the recording before repeating (Celce-Murcia et al., 2010).

Martinsen, Montgomery, and Willardson (2017) report the benefits of using tracking to improve high school students' "pronunciation performance" (i.e., accuracy of specific phonemes, general accent, word and sentence stress, and general intonation) in a French as a foreign language classroom. During the 10-week academic term, students completed a series of short (5–10 mins.) pronunciation tracking exercises, three times per week. At the start of each class period, the teacher played a short video (2–3 mins.) from the student textbook, *D'accord!* (Mitschke & Tano, 2011). As students watched the videos – captioned in both English and French – they were asked to follow along with French subtitles and track speakers as closely as they could. As a whole class, students tried to imitate what was said by reproducing the speech of both speakers in the videos as closely as they could, mimicking the speakers' accents, rhythm, and intonation, and with as little lag time as possible. There was no prior or subsequent analysis of the use of speakers' pronunciation patterns in context and no input was provided on social context or pragmatics (although the variety of social contexts portrayed in the videos was claimed by the authors to sensitize students to context-specific pragmatic factors). Students performed this tracking activity as a sort of choral repetition exercise, with the teacher stopping the video from time to time to correct student errors. However, because of the whole-class, simultaneous nature of the activity, Martinsen et al. state that it was not always possible for the teacher to hear and correct less salient pronunciation mistakes (whatever those might be). After asking students to repeat the teacher's correction, the video was resumed, and the tracking exercise continued.

Table 5.2 evaluates the tracking exercise reported in Martinsen et al. against the list of recommendations originally presented in Table 5.1 and shows that this pedagogy partially meets only two of the five recommendations for top-down pronunciation instruction. Whereas the instructor in the study showed "culturally authentic" video content (p. 673) depicting conversations in various cultural settings, presumably including non-verbal communication and pragmatics, students' attention was not drawn to these elements. Likewise, students were not asked to notice or analyze any changes to verbal or non-verbal communication patterns.

TABLE 5.2. Evaluation of Tracking Activity (Martinsen et al., 2017)

Synthesized Recommendations for Top-Down Pronunciation Instruction	Yes/No
1. Does the activity focus on unique learner goals related to pronunciation, pragmatics, and non-verbals?	No
2. Does the activity include elements of choice, agency, voice, and identity?	No
3. Does the activity emphasize communication in social context?	Partially
4. Does the activity include noticing and awareness-raising activities, controlled practice, and feedback?	Partially
5. Does the activity include application to new content and reflection?	No

Despite the general improvement in students' pronunciation that Martinsen et al. report, this in-class exercise received mixed reviews from students. Some students appreciated the consistency of beginning each class in the same way (i.e., with the tracking exercise) and found the exercises helpful due to the immediate feedback they received from the teacher. Other students, however, mentioned concerns with the noise level (students were all talking at once), not being able to hear the speakers in the video (students were talking over the video), and the fixed rate of speech (students could not control the speed of the video or the rate at which they talked, lest they fall behind in the video); a few students also described this activity as "incredibly boring" (p. 672), because of the repetitive nature and also, perhaps, because students were not able to choose the videos themselves, which would add an element of student interest and motivation. To mitigate these concerns, it's possible that shadowing (pausing the video before repeating after the speaker) might better lend itself to this type of whole-class activity; or, students could be asked to complete this activity individually or in pairs to avoid creating too much noise and talking over one another. Students could also be given the opportunity to choose the videos for themselves and complete this activity individually.

Foote and McDonough (2017) describe their use of shadowing with L2 speakers of English studying at an English-medium university in Canada. They gave students iPods that were pre-loaded with audio-recorded dialogues – all about a minute in length – taken from popular television sitcoms such as *Friends*, *How I Met Your Mother*, and *The Big Bang Theory* (among others). All of these scenes were situated within the greater context of an episode, although it is unclear whether students had viewed these episodes in their entirety or had any contextual knowledge about the episode's plot, characters, or their relationships to each other; they could only listen to the speakers, not see them, and watching the episodes via YouTube was given only as an option, not an explicit instruction. Thus, learners received no input on the speakers' social context, use of pragmatics, or non-verbals. From these pre-designated options, students could choose which audio-recordings to listen to for the shadowing activity. Students were not given strict rules for how to practice shadowing and did not receive training on speech analysis or awareness-raising activities regarding changes to pronunciation patterns in context. They were asked to practice at least four times per week for ten minutes at a time, to record themselves doing so, and to submit these recordings to the researchers for analysis. Besides these instructions, there were no other time constraints; the students could practice shadowing anytime and anywhere they chose.

Based on recordings that students created during their shadowing practice (rated by NSs for accentedness, comprehensibility, and fluency), Foote and McDonough report that all students showed overall improvement in comprehensibility and fluency, but there was no improvement in students' general accent. When students were asked their own opinions about whether they perceived the activity to be effective in improving their pronunciation, all but one answered positively, and some gave reasons for why it was effective. Students remarked, for example, on the small amount of time that was required to complete the activities and the availability to practice with authentic materials that they could select themselves. One student noted that he found this method "more useful than traditional classroom instruction" (Foote & McDonough, 2017, p. 46). As for the negative comment, this came from a student who felt the whole process was tedious and wished they could have practiced with someone instead of individually using recordings. Perhaps a video clip complemented by background on social context and storyline, and an analysis of social factors involved in each interaction, including non-verbals and pragmatics, and ideally, practice with a live interlocutor, would have improved this activity. Table 5.3 evaluates Foote and McDonough's shadowing exercise against our list of top-down teaching recommendations. This activity partially meets only two of the five recommendations, as students were given the option to practice with dialogues of their choosing between somewhat limited options (i.e., segmented dialogues from pre-selected sitcom episodes); the activity also allowed students the opportunity for a lot of controlled practice while shadowing. However, students did not receive feedback on these recordings and were not tasked with analyzing their own recordings or trained on how to do so.

TABLE 5.3. Evaluation of Shadowing Activity (Foote & McDonough, 2017)

Synthesized Recommendations for Top-Down Pronunciation Instruction	Yes/No
1. Does the activity focus on unique learner goals related to pronunciation, pragmatics, and non-verbals?	No
2. Does the activity include elements of choice, agency, voice, and identity?	Partially
3. Does the activity emphasize communication in social context?	No
4. Does the activity include noticing and awareness-raising activities, controlled practice, and feedback?	Partially
5. Does the activity include application to new content and reflection?	No

Adding an element of learner agency in a study that combines tracking and rehearsal, Henrichsen (2015) offers "video voiceovers" as a pronunciation practice activity that he describes as helpful, enjoyable, and able to increase learner motivation in pronunciation classrooms. In this activity, students are introduced to the project and asked to search online for and choose a short video clip from a movie or television scene, commercial, etc. The students have the freedom to choose whatever clip they might like, as long as it involves more than one speaker and the speakers' mouths are visible while they are talking (i.e., they are not turned away from the camera). Once students have each selected their video clips, they create a transcript and, should they decide to work in pairs or small groups, decide which character's part they will play in the video voiceover. With the help of their transcript, students play their video clip many times while tracking and pay close attention to both segmentals and suprasegmentals. While students do this, the teacher circulates to give feedback. Once students are able to track/speak along with the video clip at a normal speed, students mute the audio and continue speaking, synchronizing their speech with the characters' mouth movements and other non-verbals. Henrichsen suggests that if time allows, students should present their clips to the entire class, speaking out loud with the muted video playing behind them.

Table 5.4 evaluates Henrichsen's video voiceover exercise against the same list of top-down teaching recommendations.

TABLE 5.4. Evaluation of Video Voiceover Activity (Henrichsen, 2015)

Synthesized Recommendations for Top-Down Pronunciation Instruction	Yes/No
1. Does the activity focus on unique learner goals related to pronunciation, pragmatics, and non-verbals?	Yes
2. Does the activity include elements of choice, agency, voice, and identity?	Yes
3. Does the activity emphasize communication in social context?	Partially
4. Does the activity include noticing and awareness-raising activities, controlled practice, and feedback?	Partially
5. Does the activity include application to new content and reflection?	No

As shown in Table 5.4, this activity appears to be very adaptable to individual students and it allows students to choose a video segment that they enjoy or feel some kind of connection to. Unfortunately, though, this technique does not explicitly draw students' attention to the social factors influencing the communicative context or include noticing or awareness-raising activities where students analyze changes to the verbal and non-verbal communication patterns, therefore only partially meeting the third and fourth recommendations. It also does not include application to new content or reflection beyond the final performance of the voiceover that Henrichsen recommends.

Following close to the same "tracking and rehearsal" procedure as video voiceovers, Huang and Tseng (2021) report on the positive effects of L2 students' successful "film-dubbing" at a university in Taiwan. In their classroom exploration study, Huang and Tseng assigned students both individual and group dubbing tasks. For each task, students did not choose their own videos, as in Henrichsen (2015), but were able to choose from one of eight pre-selected video recordings taken from one of four English films (i.e., *Atonement*, *The Curious Case of Benjamin Button*, *You've Got Mail*, and *While You Were Sleeping*). For the individual dubbing activity, students selected a monologue; for the group activity, they selected a dialogue between characters. Besides limiting students' choice, Huang and Tseng's description of film-dubbing also differs from Henrichsen's video voiceovers in that it includes the expression of emotion within the communicative context of the speaking event. Huang and Tseng (2021) describe the movie scenes as being spoken "at a slower pace and with feelings and emotion" (p. 2). In order for students to add emotions to their voice for successful film-dubbing, they first have to understand and analyze the emotions being portrayed. The authors do not explicitly state that analysis focused on expression of emotion was included in the sequence of activities involved in film-dubbing, but one could infer that teachers would spend some time talking about the emotions that characters are experiencing in the film. Table 5.5 evaluates the film-dubbing exercise reported in Huang and Tseng using our synthesized top-down teaching recommendations. Whereas students are given limited choice between several scenes to analyze and perform for the activity (thus partially meeting the second recommendation of choice, agency, voice, and identity), there is a lack of focus on how these scenes related to individual learners' goals related to pronunciation, pragmatics, and non-verbals. Moreover, this activity also neglects to include any kind of application to new content or student reflection.

TABLE 5.5. Evaluation of Film-Dubbing Activity (Huang & Tseng, 2021)

Synthesized Recommendations for Top-Down Pronunciation Instruction	Yes/No
1. Does the activity focus on unique learner goals related to pronunciation, pragmatics, and non-verbals?	No
2. Does the activity include elements of choice, agency, voice, and identity?	Partially
3. Does the activity emphasize communication in social context?	Yes
4. Does the activity include noticing and awareness-raising activities, controlled practice, and feedback?	Yes
5. Does the activity include application to new content and reflection?	No

Finally, in the appendix to their course book for teaching pronunciation, Celce-Murcia et al. (2010, pp. 489–490) offer one sample activity, called "A Dramatic Imitative Approach," which uses a blend of tracking and shadowing and which starts with an analysis of social context and pragmatics. Using a short video clip that the teacher chooses for the students depicting scenes from films or television sitcoms (the authors give the examples of *Seinfeld* and *Friends*, not unlike Foote and McDonough), the teacher moves through five steps:

1. **Analysis**: Students view the clip first without sound and try to predict what is happening in the scene. Looking at non-verbal communication patterns such as gesture, facial expression, and distance between speakers, students try to guess what kind of relationship characters have with one another and what their attitudes or emotions are. After viewing the video clip a second time – this time with sound – students confirm or correct their predictions. Later, the teacher gives students a transcript of the scene and students are asked to again predict instances of pausing, prominence, and intonation. After completing this individually, the teacher plays the video line by line and draws students' attention to these prosodic elements while also highlighting changes in facial expression and gesture, and students revise their transcripts accordingly. Finally, the whole class discusses the underlying pragmatic meaning of the lines.

2. **Imitation and Rehearsal**: In the second step, students rehearse the scene. The teacher plays the video line by line and students practice imitating these lines in a choral repetition. Later, they are put into pairs to practice reading from their transcript, imitating the speakers' pronunciation and non-verbals. The teacher circulates and gives feedback to groups.

3. **Performance**: After practicing with the transcript, students perform the scene in pairs and these performances are recorded. Following their performance, students receive a role-play prompt which describes a situation similar to the scene they practiced, and they are asked to transfer these same prosodic features to the new role-play, which is also recorded.

4. **Evaluation**: In the final step, students review and evaluate their recordings – both of the original scene and of the role-play. The teacher also views the video recordings and gives students feedback on their pronunciation.

Although this teaching technique was presented in Celce-Murcia et al. without any account of how teachers and students have actually used this in L2 classrooms, the step-by-step description of the activities and choice of materials appears promising for including important factors of social context and IL pragmatics. However, it still seems to neglect any emphasis on the impact of learner identity and choice as it relates to L2 phonology, and it does not fully lend itself to address students' unique goals related to pronunciation, pragmatics, and non-verbals (as all students analyzed and performed the same video). Table 5.6 evaluates Celce-Murcia et al.'s teaching technique against the list of top-down teaching recommendations. To better fulfill these synthesized recommendations, teachers might allow students to choose their own speech models and video clips, which could greatly improve this activity.

TABLE 5.6. Evaluation of A Dramatic Imitative Approach (Celce-Murcia et al., 2010)

Synthesized Recommendations for Top-Down Pronunciation Instruction	Yes/No
1. Does the activity focus on unique learner goals related to pronunciation, pragmatics, and non-verbals?	Partially
2. Does the activity include elements of choice, agency, voice, and identity?	No
3. Does the activity emphasize communication in social context?	Yes
4. Does the activity include noticing and awareness-raising activities, controlled practice, and feedback?	Yes
5. Does the activity include application to new content and reflection?	Yes

From each of the described tracking or shadowing activities, it appears that there are clear pedagogical benefits to these types of top-down pedagogies. For studies that included some kind of measurement to document students' pronunciation improvement over time (e.g., Foote & McDonough, 2017; Huang & Tseng, 2021; Martinsen et al., 2017), each of these tracking or shadowing activities was successful and the majority of students reported that they enjoyed doing them. The only negative comments came from students who either felt that the tracking exercises were repetitive or boring, or wished they had a partner to practice with instead of a recording. In critique of these activities, we underscore the importance of learner agency in choosing materials that align with students' unique goals and interests for improving pronunciation and that reflect the identity(ies) they would like to maintain and/or construct in the L2 as well as the voices they wish to internalize. We also highlight the importance of training in advance, particularly analyzing the social situational factors, emotion, and underlying pragmatics in any of the materials that teachers use for tracking or shadowing. Understanding a speaker's emotion and the pragmatic context of speaking is central to knowing how to position the prosodic elements of an utterance and how to say what to whom, when. Finally, we have critiqued many of these activities for not asking students to reflect on what they have learned or to apply it to new content or performances. In the following section, we review drama-based methods that do begin with an analysis of these factors and which include reflection and carryover to new content.

Drama Technique Pedagogies

Galante and Thomson (2017) provide a helpful distinction between the terms *theatre techniques* and *drama techniques*. Theatre techniques are product-oriented and as such emphasize pre-established roles, scripted language, and a final staged delivery of a performance by students. Examples of these techniques can be found in many L2 textbooks that include more or less "authentic" dialogues that students are asked to act out and perform, though little is said about social factors that may influence students' portrayal of the characters in these dramas. Drama techniques, like role-play, are improvisational and process-oriented and emphasize the experience of the dramatic task at hand. In these activities, students may be asked to work in groups and negotiate meaning related to the given (or student-created) situation, create new characters or personae for themselves, and improvise dialogue with more natural or extemporaneous speech.

Drama techniques have long been argued to promote L2 learners' development of oral communication skills and speaking fluency. Stern (1980), for example, explored the impact of using drama techniques in advanced ESL classes and found that such an approach to teaching resulted in students' increased self-esteem, motivation, and spontaneity in speaking. Kao (1994), too, looked at how drama techniques promoted classroom interaction among L2 learners of English in Taiwan; she found that this type of instruction gave students more opportunity to use English in class, thus indirectly supporting and promoting their fluency in speaking. Coleman (2005) and Stinson and Freebody (2006) have argued similar benefits to using a drama approach to teaching for improving learners' oral communication – in the most general sense – in Korean and Singaporean contexts, respectively.

Drama techniques have also been used in the development of ITA programs and other resources in response to the influx of international graduate teaching assistants in the United States to help NNS students improve their intelligibility (e.g., Acton, 1984; Hinofotis & Bailey, 1978; Mestenhauser, Perry, Paige, Landa, Brutsch, Dege, Doyle, Gillette, Hughes, Judy, Keye, Murphy, Smith, Vandersluis, & Wendt, 1980; S. Stevens, 1989). One of the best examples is described by S. Stevens (1989) as an intelligibility program, implemented at the University of Delaware, which consisted of a 40-hour course that adapted role-play and other drama techniques to ITA training. Citing top-down research such as that of Guiora et al. (1972, reviewed in Chapter 3), Stevens offers a pedagogical program that cut across three distinct components: language training with a focus on suprasegmentals, cultural training, and pedagogical training. To combine all three parts of this class, ITAs were encouraged to engage in whole-body role-plays and other drama techniques in order to create a "mask" that they could adopt when performing their teaching roles. For Stevens, teachers are like actors in that they, too, must learn to read their audience to know the extent to which their message is being appropriately conveyed and understood. Stevens claims that self-conscious ITAs respond well to this idea of a figurative mask because they can take on a new role "and 'become' a different, more confident other" (S. Stevens, 1989, p. 186).

S. Stevens (1989) applies drama methods from "The Lessac System" (Lessac, 1967), which emphasizes the physical aspect of voice and encourages students' analysis of how particular words and sounds should FEEL for the speaker. In so doing, this class addresses several important skills (cf. S. Stevens, 1989, pp. 188–190):

1. **Group Development**: to build trust between the instructor(s), the ITAs, and their students in the classroom, Stevens used activities such as team chants, circles of trust, and sharing personal experiences.
2. **Stage Voice**: to teach projection, linking, reductions, intonation, and rhythm, example activities included tracking the speech of American students and choral chants to practice linking and reductions.
3. **Observation and Movement**: to master non-verbal language, to move (and speak) like NSs while using culturally appropriate facial expressions and gestures, ITAs were assigned to observe American professors teaching and to take careful notes. Later, they attempted to recreate these actions themselves.

4. **Energy**: to project confidence to the audience; speaking with power and energy, students practiced projecting their voice by having discussions from across the room (30 feet away) and "controlled shouting matches."

5. **Concentration**: to learn how to keep the mask on and not slip back into previous habits, students practiced concentration with activities that asked them to assume and maintain characters in various mini dramas or practice holding three-way conversations, all while gliding through mistakes (not stumbling over them).

6. **Spontaneity and Creativity**: to make their lines appear natural when donning a mask, ITAs tried to capitalize on any humorous moments and provide necessary reformulations or explanations when students appeared confused. Some sample activities described are "the hard push" (challenging ITAs at nearly every statement, forcing them to move beyond their originally planned script) and improvisation activities such as debate.

7. **Mechanics**: to control the space ITAs take up in a room, in classroom activities, they practice entrances, exits, and how to maximize their use of the full teaching area.

To help these "actors-in-training" (i.e., ITAs) learn their new role and become more familiar with their audience, U.S. undergraduates were employed to interact with the ITAs throughout the activities and across these skill areas as "coaches, speech and gesture models, vocabulary and slang sources, and co-performers in various mini performances that were reviewed and critiqued" (S. Stevens, 1989, p. 187). In addition to these undergraduate student coaches, the program also provided each student with a trained ESL professional as a language tutor who could also choose to assign ITAs additional homework to practice suprasegmental or segmental features of their English, depending on their unique needs for pronunciation improvement.

A year-long evaluation (confirmed by three different proficiency measurements) found that this 40-hour course significantly improved the oral intelligibility of the international graduate students. ITAs, too, reported in their self-evaluations that they believed they made much progress in improving their suprasegmentals. Table 5.7 uses our list of top-down teaching recommendations to evaluate Steven's intelligibility program. As shown in Table 5.7, this program does an excellent job at meeting our identified criteria, especially with regard to our third and fifth recommendations. Stevens' use of a live audience drawn from the

ITAs' target population of U.S. undergraduates is an important addition to this program that invites application to new content and reflection.

TABLE 5.7. Evaluation of Intelligibility Program (S. Stevens, 1989)

Synthesized Recommendations for Top-Down Pronunciation Instruction	Yes/No
1. Does the activity focus on unique learner goals related to pronunciation, pragmatics, and non-verbals?	Yes
2. Does the activity include elements of choice, agency, voice, and identity?	Yes
3. Does the activity emphasize communication in social context?	Yes
4. Does the activity include noticing and awareness-raising activities, controlled practice, and feedback?	Yes
5. Does the activity include application to new content and reflection?	Yes

In another study focusing on role-play, Morgan (1997) describes using similar drama techniques for immigrants in an adult basic education program which explored ways to relate the sound system of English to its use in social interaction and to students' evolving identity(ies) and emotion. Morgan asked his students, adult newcomers from Hong Kong, to reflect on their past experiences and revaluate them in the context of their present situation(s), asking how the "rules of identity" shift from one context to another, impacting students' new and old traditions, present relationships and interactions, and important life goals for the future. Drawing on Halliday's (1985) social-semiotic approach to language, which views language not as an isolated grammar system of rules and patterns but as a social resource for construing meaning, Morgan drew students' attention to how the smallest linguistic units (including prosodic elements such as rhythm and intonation) could be explained in relation to larger social contextual variables to reflect the specific functions of language intended for a given situation. Citing Kreidler (1989, p. 156), Morgan provides a nice example of this by applying thought group boundaries (marked by an upward slash) in two different ways:

> / we don't want any /
> / we / don't / want / any /

In the second utterance, there is a slight pause between every word and the speaker places equal stress on each syllable; in the context of speaking, this pattern might be used to emphasize displeasure or irritation (perhaps after initially refusing the unknown interlocutor's offer several times prior!). Understanding this function of rhythm is important, but Morgan encourages teachers not to stop at function. He addresses the danger of teaching prosody, for instance, as a specific form-function relationship, preferring to encourage students to dig deeper into the context of identity and expression by having them ask three important questions as they analyze speech samples and use role-plays: (1) Who is speaking? (2) Why are they having this conversation? (3) What language will help them achieve their purpose? Thus, not only is Morgan encouraging students to think about the language used in dramatic re-enactment, as they did in S. Stevens' (1989) work; he is also connecting the teaching of suprasegmentals to their use in social interaction. By drawing learners' attention to the meaning reflected by changes to discrete linguistic units, what Morgan is really doing is giving students a more detailed understanding of the power language has to shape and reflect the underlying pragmatics of the situation as well as speakers' emotions and social identities.

Foregrounding these issues of social power and identity work, Morgan described a sample lesson titled "Isolation," which began with a short reading and moved into a role-play activity with a focus on intonation, specifically. In this lesson, his students (all newcomers from Hong Kong) read about a problem facing "Yuen-Li," a Chinese immigrant living in the United States whose husband was very traditionally minded and believed she should stay at home to mind the house and children. She felt very isolated and wanted to learn English (as she only spoke Cantonese), but she worried what her husband would say or do if she told him this. After reading the passage, the class discussed and ranked appropriate solutions for Yuen-Li's problem, and the next day Morgan returned with a scripted dialogue that incorporated some of the students' ideas (highlighting some important elements of student choice and agency) for a role-play activity. Looking at each sentence one by one, the teacher asked the students what emotions and feelings would emerge naturally in a conversation between the husband and wife if, for example, Yuen-Li took English classes without her husband's knowledge and only told him after she learned to speak English. How would the husband communicate his surprise via intonation patterns? How many different meanings could be communicated by only changing the tone and intonation of the word *oh*? How might Yuen-Li most effectively negotiate her new evolving identity and future life goals with her husband, and what elements of this would be reflected in her intonation patterns? After identifying, marking, and practicing these patterns as a whole class, students then created their own (new) dialogues about the same imagined scenario between Yuen-Li and her husband or another family member, such as her son. After again thinking carefully about what intonation patterns would be most appropriate and effective for the given context of speaking, students presented these role-plays in front of the class.

Table 5.8 evaluates Morgan's role-play activity in terms of our list of top-down teaching recommendations. As shown in Table 5.8, this activity meets many of the criteria we identify for effective top-down L2 pronunciation teaching techniques. In order to fully meet the second recommendation, thereby fulfilling all five of these synthesized recommendations, Morgan might have allowed students to choose their own situational context to analyze, either in the first place or following the whole group discussion, instead of all students' analyzing the problem that Yuen-Li faced in the lesson "Isolation." He also might have provided examples of possible accompanying non-verbals that would fit the situational context of speaking and thereby fully meet the first recommendation, now only partially met. Morgan does not go into detail about students' opinions regarding this lesson or its effectiveness for teaching intonation patterns (students' ability to understand and produce these patterns was not measured *per se*), but it is clear that this lesson facilitated students' greater understanding of how sentence-level stress patterns and intonation can serve as a resource for negotiating identity and (re)defining social relationships.

TABLE 5.8. Evaluation of Role-Play Activity (Morgan, 1997)

Synthesized Recommendations for Top-Down Pronunciation Instruction	Yes/No
1. Does the activity focus on unique learner goals related to pronunciation, pragmatics, and non-verbals?	Partially
2. Does the activity include elements of choice, agency, voice, and identity?	Partially
3. Does the activity emphasize communication in social context?	Yes
4. Does the activity include noticing and awareness-raising activities, controlled practice, and feedback?	Yes
5. Does the activity include application to new content and reflection?	Yes

As described in the aforementioned studies (e.g., Morgan, 1997; Stern, 1980; S. Stevens, 1989), drama techniques have been shown to promote L2 learners' development of oral communication skills, speaking fluency, and intelligibility. However, these studies can be critiqued for not being able to demonstrate any kind of causal relationship between process drama approaches and L2 learning (cf. Galante & Thomson, 2017, p.

120). Applying a more fine-grained analysis, Galante and Thomson (2017) respond to this critique and report on a study documenting changes to L2 students' fluency, comprehensibility, and accentedness as a direct result of drama-based teaching within a traditional English language classroom in Brazil. In this quasi-experimental study, an experimental and a control classroom (located at two different sites of the same language institute) were included for analysis to estimate the causal impact of the dramatic intervention. In the control group, the class followed a communicative, task-based approach to language teaching with an added component on pronunciation using a bottom-up approach. This group focused on contrastive analysis of consonant and vowel sounds as well as suprasegmental features that were known to be challenging for Portuguese speakers learning English. Students were asked to listen and repeat strings of words and sentences, and also complete tracking exercises as they followed along to the transcripts of audio passages. In contrast to this more traditional model of teaching, the experimental group followed a top-down drama-based program consisting of both process-oriented and product-oriented approaches to working on pronunciation improvement. In this top-down program, drama-based and regular English language activities from the course textbook were blended together. Galante and Thomson (2017, p. 123) give an example of this using a textbook unit on descriptive adjectives. To complement this unit, drama activities were designed so students could practice these same lexical units through improvised simulations, role-plays, and problem-solving games that required them to notice what phonological elements needed to be applied in order to correctly communicate their intended meaning. In addition to this process-oriented blended approach, students also completed various scripted scenarios and role-plays, rehearsing these scenes before performing them in front of the class.

To measure students' improvement after four months of instruction, both the experimental and control group completed a series of speaking tasks that served as pretests and posttests. These speaking tasks asked students to describe a picture story, watch and retell the plot of a short video, perform a role-play, perform a monologue, and then repeat again the first picture story only now using a different subject pronoun (i.e., changing it from third to first person or vice versa). Thirty untrained raters (NSs of English who had never studied Portuguese), listened to 20-second excerpts from each of these speaking tasks and rated students on their fluency, comprehensibility, and accentedness. Results demonstrate a significant difference in fluency and comprehensibility between the experimental and control group, with the experimental group making larger gains on average in fluency and comprehensibility than the control group. In terms of accent, both groups appeared to make modest improvements, but they did so with no statistical difference between the two groups.

Research showed these drama-based pedagogical materials were effective in improving students' oral comprehensibility and fluency, which are the goals of a top-down approach to pronunciation instruction, rather than to rid students of their accents. Table 5.9 evaluates the drama-based quasi-experimental study reported in Galante and Thomson using our synthesized top-down teaching recommendations. In application of these recommendations to the drama techniques described in this study, it is not clear whether students were given a choice between several scenes to analyze or perform for the activity (and thus this only partially meets our recommendation); there is also a lack of focus on individual learners' goals related to pronunciation, pragmatics, and non-verbals.

TABLE 5.9. Evaluation of Drama-Based Experimental Study (Galante & Thomson, 2017)

Synthesized Recommendations for Top-Down Pronunciation Instruction	Yes/No
1. Does the activity focus on unique learner goals related to pronunciation, pragmatics, and non-verbals?	No
2. Does the activity include elements of choice, agency, voice, and identity?	Partially
3. Does the activity emphasize communication in social context?	Yes
4. Does the activity include noticing and awareness-raising activities, controlled practice, and feedback?	Yes
5. Does the activity include application to new content and reflection?	Yes

In consideration of the teaching methods and techniques so far presented in S. Stevens (1989), Morgan (1997), and Galante and Thomson (2017), it appears that drama techniques have been successful in their inclusion of many of the recommendations we give for top-down L2 pronunciation instruction, and research has shown that they improve learners' comprehensibility. So, what materials and techniques are readily available for teachers who might want to implement such programs in their own classrooms and who do not already have a background in theater or the wherewithal to create their own materials?

Finger (1999) and Carkin (2005a, 2007; Carkin, Hall, & Day, 2003) have responded to a call for readily available drama-based materials for ESL purposes by collecting and/or creating resources for practicing teachers who wish to incorporate a drama-based approach in their classroom but do not know where to start. Applying a drama-based approach specifically to the teaching of pronunciation, Carkin (2004, 2005b) describes a series of seven steps that he takes with his students at Southern New Hampshire University in a drama course that has been fully integrated into the ESL curriculum.

1. **Teach students basic transcription markings and a phonetic alphabet** (such as the International Phonetic Alphabet [IPA]). Students should learn how to mark for suprasegmental elements such as pausing, word or sentence stress, intonation contours, and a system like IPA for segmentals so that when the teacher makes a correction to students' pronunciation during the drama process, they can take the notes and practice.

2. **Present play options to the students.** The teacher selects a few short plays (15 minutes or less) that students can read through and understand quickly, ideally during a single class period, while leaving enough time for discussion (see Carkin, 2005a; Carkin et al., 2003 for examples of such plays). Asking students to choose the play they are most interested in is important for student motivation and buy-in to the process.

3. **Students discuss the plays and the characters they identify with.** Students can share what they found interesting about the plays, and which they would be most interested in performing. Students should also take this time to discuss characters and see if they especially resonate (i.e., identify) with any of the character roles or motives. The fact that students choose a character that they identify with is key to their "becoming" that character, although it is not clear what happens if multiple students wish to play the same character in a play.

4. **Students make a final decision on the play and characters and form small groups.** In these groups, students discuss the objective of their play and what motivates their characters. Students should also analyze their scripts for clues about the emotions and temperament of their characters – what do they feel and why do they feel that way? How will these emotions impact the pronunciation patterns that students need to perform? Acting

as a coach, the teacher listens to students read their lines out loud and gives feedback on their pronunciation and performance.

5. **Students develop an "inner monologue" for their characters.** Students use the few clues they can glean from the script and, with the help of their imagination, create a detailed backstory for their characters. This allows learners to further connect and identify with their character roles and develop their character's subtext. What is the character thinking as they deliver their lines? What is their intention and what language cues or prosodic elements do students need to apply to make this clear to the audience?

6. **Students rehearse their lines using the "look and speak" method with their character's subtext in mind.** As students first read their lines, they pause and then look up before they speak during rehearsal; the teacher gives immediate feedback on pronunciation. Carkin argues that this leads students to play themselves, as they were the ones who created this intricate backstory.

7. **Add movement.** Once students have memorized their lines, they add movement and other forms of non-verbal communication. Some of these moves are roughly blocked out in the script already, but details are very minimal. Acting as the director, the teacher helps position students and explain any culturally unique meanings about movements or gestures. Finally, students are ready to perform their play in front of an audience of their teacher and their peers. There is no mention of a final reflection or application of students' character voices to new contexts.

Table 5.10 evaluates Carkin's (2004, 2005b) ESL drama course for pronunciation purposes against the list of top-down teaching recommendations we provide in this chapter. As shown in Table 5.10, this drama course meets most of the criteria we have identified in our recommendations; the only activities it neglects to include are any kind of application to new content, or student reflection following the performance of the play.

Drama techniques, like those presented here, can be very helpful for NNS students working to overcome a lack of confidence in speaking English (e.g., Kao, 1994; Stern, 1980) and also significantly improve students' L2 fluency and comprehensibility (Galante & Thomson, 2017). Students who train in drama to improve their intelligibility may find ample opportunities to carry these techniques over into their everyday speech as they consider what emotion or intention they need to convey in a given social context and analyze how they can clearly communicate this through their use of suprasegmentals. ITAs, especially, in the dual role of teacher-actors, can make full use of such techniques and their new found voice and movement if they can accept S. Stevens' (1989) proposition that the classroom is their theater and the American undergraduate student, their audience.

TABLE 5.10. Evaluation of the ESL Drama Course (Carkin, 2004, 2005b)

Synthesized Recommendations for Top-Down Pronunciation Instruction	Yes/No
1. Does the activity focus on unique learner goals related to pronunciation, pragmatics, and non-verbals?	Yes
2. Does the activity include elements of choice, agency, voice, and identity?	Yes
3. Does the activity emphasize communication in social context?	Yes
4. Does the activity include noticing and awareness-raising activities, controlled practice, and feedback?	Yes
5. Does the activity include application to new content and reflection?	No

Review of Top-Down Pedagogies

In Table 5.11, we summarize the information presented above in Tables 5.2–5.10 to provide an overview of how all of these top-down pedagogies meet the recommendations for best practice in Table 5.1.

As shown in Table 5.11, it appears that *Recommendation 5: Application to New Content and Reflection* is the LEAST common among these teaching methods, followed by *Recommendation 1: Focus on Unique Learner Goals for Intelligibility: Pronunciation, Pragmatics, and Non-Verbals* and *Recommendation 2: Elements of Choice, Agency, Voice, and Identity in Students' Learning*. Situating the activities in social and communicative context, highlighting the influence of situational factors such as the speaker's purpose, emotion, and interlocutor/audience (*Recommendation 3: Emphasis on Communication in Social Context*), appears to be more common among the activities presented in this chapter; and most common by far is *Recommendation 4: Noticing and Awareness-Raising Activities, Controlled Practice, and Feedback*. Not shown clearly in Table 5.11 is S. Stevens' (1989) innovative use of a live audience drawn from the learners' target population to approximate real-world application and stimulate reflection.

TABLE 5.11. Summary of Top-Down Pedagogies and Synthesized Recommendations

Synthesized Recommendations for Top-Down Instruction	Martinsen et al., 2017	Foote & McDonough, 2017	Henrichsen, 2015	Huang & Tseng, 2021	Celce-Murcia et al., 2010	S. Stevens, 1989	Morgan, 1997	Galante & Thomson, 2017	Carkin, 2004, 2005b
1. Does the activity focus on unique learner goals related to pronunciation, pragmatics, and non-verbals?	No	No	Yes	No	Partially	Yes	Partially	No	Yes
2. Does the activity include elements of choice, agency, voice, and identity?	No	Partially	Yes	Partially	No	Yes	Partially	Partially	Yes
3. Does the activity emphasize communication in social context?	Partially	No	Partially	Yes	Yes	Yes	Yes	Yes	Yes
4. Does the activity include noticing and awareness-raising activities, controlled practice, and feedback?	Partially	Partially	Partially	Yes	Yes	Yes	Yes	Yes	Yes
5. Does the activity include application to new content and reflection?	No	No	No	No	Yes	Yes	Yes	Yes	No

In review of these recommendations, we would like to remind readers of the importance of differentiating instruction to meet the unique needs of students from different language backgrounds, past learning contexts, and interactional experiences; such different learners can have vastly different areas of focus for pronunciation improvement when it comes to intelligibility, let alone identity, emotion, and pragmatic goals. It is important to emphasize the benefit of providing students with choice/agency in their learning. As we have argued extensively in this book (see Chapters 1, 2, 3, and 4), pronunciation and accent are inextricably tied to expressions of speaker identity, and students' use of materials and methods in learning should reflect the identity(ies) and voices they would like to maintain and/or construct in the L2. It is our recommendation that students apply what they have learned in new contexts, ideally in their target speech community, and then that they be given the opportunity to reflect on what they have learned and how well they have met their unique goals to overcome specific challenges with pronunciation, pragmatics, and non-verbals.

Chapter 5 in Review

In this chapter, we have built upon the previous work of other scholars (e.g., Douglas Fir Group, 2016; Moyer, 2017; Müller, 2013; Pennington & Richards, 1986; Yates, 2017) to create a synthesized list of general teaching recommendations for top-down pronunciation instruction (see Table 5.1 shown on page 69). Applying this list to the context of various teaching activities, we have described in detail the use of contextualized and authentic or adapted materials which employ a top-down approach to teaching pronunciation, including those engaging such methods as tracking and shadowing as well as role-play and other drama techniques, and have evaluated these activities against our set of synthesized recommendations. We ended the chapter with Table 5.11, which compares the features of all of the top-down approaches reviewed in the chapter as they relate to the recommendations presented in Table 5.1.

In the following chapter (Chapter 6), we present the Mirroring Project: an effective top-down pedagogical approach for L2 pronunciation instruction which not only meets all five of our synthesized recommendations, but also helps learners internalize and then use for their own purposes the voices (including non-verbals) of self-selected role models. As students work towards meeting their own unique goals in pronunciation, pragmatics, and identity expression, they select and re-enact the voices of video-recorded speakers they have chosen, focusing on their identity expression, emotion, and pragmatic goals. Following their analysis and attempt to move and speak like their selected model, students "channel" that voice – the discursive, non-verbal, and pragmatic features of their model – to deliver their own messages and reflect on what it feels like to speak to their target audience with that voice, to improve their intelligibility, delivery, and expression of identity in their target speech community.

Chapter 6

The Mirroring Project

Introduction to Mirroring

As we have seen in Chapter 5, top-down approaches to pronunciation instruction share several characteristics in common. Building on the work of other scholars (e.g., Moyer, 2017; Müller, 2013; Pennington & Richards, 1986; Yates, 2017), we synthesized these common characteristics into the following list of recommendations for effective top-down pronunciation instruction:

1. Focus on unique learner goals for intelligibility: pronunciation, pragmatics, and non-verbals.
2. Provide elements of choice, agency, voice, and identity in students' learning.
3. Emphasize communication in social context.
4. Include noticing and awareness-raising activities, controlled practice, and feedback.
5. Ask learners to apply learned material to new content, followed by reflection on their own performance.

As we will show, the Mirroring Project (MP) follows these recommendations and helps students to integrate linguistic and discursive aspects of L2 pronunciation with non-verbal communication and pragmatic expressions by inviting them to internalize and speak with the voices of self-selected others – where "voice," discussed in Chapter 4, is understood to be a complex of linguistic and non-verbal features signaling a speaker's emotion, social stance, and identity (Tarone, 2019; Wertsch, 1991, 2002).

In *mirroring*, students not only repeat or imitate speech and its verbal characteristics, but also emulate distinct characteristics of the physical body – creating a mirror image. The MP helps students to internalize video-recorded voices by asking them to focus on the way their chosen speaker's pronunciation (both segmental and prosodic), their non-verbal communication patterns, and their pragmatic expressions work in synchrony to convey that speaker's identity, emotion, and intended meaning. In doing so, the MP extends beyond the scope of our five recommendations to improve both intelligibility and identity expression by helping students to internalize a new voice as a composite of pronunciation, non-verbals, and pragmatics.

The MP (originally termed "The Imitation Project," in which students imitated someone whom they admired) was developed in 2001 by M. Monk at Bellevue Community College in Washington State. Monk taught students in an intensive English language program and progressively used three stages of evolution of the project. In the first version of the project, students were video-recorded teaching a pronunciation feature, which they had either learned in the course or developed themselves, to a fellow student as a way to demonstrate self-awareness and how to modify their "accent." In the next version, based on the recommendation from the Director of International Student Programs (himself an L2 speaker of English), the students undertook an "Intonation Project" in which they imitated the intonation of someone they admired. In the final version, one of the students that semester suggested having students do an initial "mini-project," in which they would do an imitation without having had any training in prosody and then a final project in which they would demonstrate what they had learned. The students would not use a marked transcript for the mini-project, but they would for the final project. Monk developed a set of guiding questions which would help students use the project as a way to develop their critical thinking skills.

At the 36th annual TESOL International Convention and English Language Expo (henceforth "TESOL Convention") in 2002, Monk presented this Imitation Project. Lindgren and Meyers attended that presentation and expressed interest in adapting the project with ITAs in mind (see Chapters 2 and 3 for discussion of ITA programming) to help them prepare for planned presentations, such as university lectures in English, their L2. The needs of this group of learners led to a focus on the use of suprasegmentals and gesture to intelligibly convey complex meaning and pragmatic intent in planned speech (Lindgren, Meyers, & Monk, 2003; Meyers, 2013, 2014; Tarone & Meyers, 2018). Lindgren et al. first presented this adaptation of the Imitation Project, which they called *mirroring*, at the 2003 TESOL Convention.

Since that initial development, the MP has undergone several changes. In 2004, Monk, Lindgren, and Meyers again presented their work on mirroring at the TESOL Convention in a presentation called "Documenting Prosodic Acquisition with the Mirroring Technique" (Monk, Lindgren, &

Meyers, 2004). They showed a video of a Mandarin speaker ("Chen," a pseudonym) who imitated Jack Nicholson in a scene from *One Flew Over the Cuckoo's Nest* (M. Forman, 1975). Two videos were shown, one in which Chen mirrored Jack Nicholson without previous analysis or marking of the transcript (as was suggested by Monk's student back in 2001), and a second in which Chen mirrored Jack Nicholson using a transcript marked for prosody and in which he paid attention to non-verbal communication. Lindgren et al. also presented a five-point evaluation rubric which included the categories of rhythm (stress, pausing, and intonation), voice (volume), articulation, non-verbal expression, and presentation (memorization, naturalness, etc.). In 2013, based on a recommendation in Murphy's (2012) TESOL Convention presentation (later published in *System*; Murphy, 2014), that "samples of [NNS] speech are useful as pronunciation models as long as they are intelligible and comprehensible" (Murphy, 2014, p. 258), Meyers' TESOL presentation entitled "Mirroring Project Update" showed a video of a student called "Mary" (pseudonym) at several stages of the MP as she imitated the speech and non-verbals of an English presentation by a NS of Mandarin who fit Murphy's criteria (Meyers, 2013). Finally, Meyers (2018) and Tarone, LaScotte, Meyers, and Moreno (2018) presented videos at the TESOL Convention and the American Association for Applied Linguistics Conference of ITAs who not only mirrored model speakers of English, but also "channeled" those speakers; that is, they embodied those models' voices to communicate their own ideas. In *channeling*, the students emulated the speech and non-verbal features and style of their model speaker to embody the model's stance in delivering the students' own words. The most recent research has shown that this approach can effectively improve correlates of intelligibility and delivery (LaScotte, 2022; LaScotte & Tarone, in press; Meyers, 2013; Tarone & Meyers, 2018). This latest version of the MP uses a top-down pedagogical approach that teaches a learner to internalize a speaker's voice with its unique patterns of pronunciation, non-verbal and pragmatic expressions, and to use those features to signal the learner's identity, stance, relational power, and communicative intent in delivery of their own original content.

In the next section, we describe ten pedagogical steps for implementing the MP to make it possible for teachers to use this approach in their own classrooms. After providing these instructions, we will show in detail how these steps were successfully implemented with two focal students who had different learning needs.

The Mirroring Project in 10 Steps

The Mirroring Project comprises three phases, broken down into 10 steps which can be undertaken over a period of about three weeks or more, depending on the available class and practice time. In what follows, we provide a list of those 10 steps, first with short descriptions to provide the reader with an overview (see Table 6.1), and then with more detailed descriptions of each step to ensure the reader can carry out such a project in their own teaching or research.

TABLE 6.1. The Mirroring Project in 10 Steps

Analysis Phase	
Step 1	In conjunction with the instructor, students identify their pronunciation and non-verbal challenges.
Step 2	Students choose a model speaker they identify with and select a short (one-to-two minute long) video-recorded speech sample.
Step 3	Students analyze their model's speech sample and non-verbals for communicative effectiveness (i.e., speaker's intent and goal) using guiding questions provided by the instructor.
Step 4	Students transcribe their speech sample, identifying and marking for thought groups, prominence, and intonation and adding annotations for non-verbal communication.
Mirroring Phase	
Step 5	Students mirror their model one thought group at a time as they follow their original video recording.
Step 6	Students practice internalizing their model's speech patterns and non-verbal communication features using the "Read, Look Up, and Say" technique.
Step 7	Students are video-recorded during a trial version, speaking to an audience of classmates and the instructor.
Step 8	Students critique the trial version with their instructor, then continue to practice improving their speech patterns and non-verbal communication features as many times as they wish.
Step 9	Students are video-recorded a final time, in front of an audience of classmates and their instructor and analyze and critique the final version.
Channeling Phase	
Step 10	Students write material for the "channeling" stage of the project, where they practice emulating the speech and non-verbal features and style of the model speaker they mirrored, but now delivering ORIGINAL content. Then, students and their instructor evaluate that channeling performance.

The three phases of the current version of the MP are *Analysis*, *Mirroring*, and *Channeling*. The *Analysis* phase involves four steps: students explicitly set learning goals for oral communication; choose a speaker they would like to emulate; select and analyze a short video-recording by that speaker to identify its purpose, pronunciation features, and non-verbal patterns; and explicitly predict possible challenges they might have in mirroring that speech sample.

1. **Identification of Pronunciation and Non-Verbal Challenges.** To explicitly identify their own challenges in pronunciation and non-verbals in speaking English as their L2, students undertake a diagnostic, such as giving a brief self-introduction, giving a short speech about a topic of interest, and/or engaging in a diagnostic interview. The diagnostic is recorded and then analyzed by the instructor and the student. Areas of interest in such an analysis might include: use of pausing, speech rate, pitch range, and non-verbal elements such as gestures. Each student, in conjunction with the instructor, comes up with a plan for improvement of pronunciation and non-verbals based on the diagnostic analysis.

2. **Selection of an Appropriate Model.** To communicate more effectively, students choose a segment of speech produced by a model speaker (NS or, as Murphy, 2014 recommends, a highly intelligible, comprehensible NNS) based not only on that speaker's identity in relation to their own, but also based on the speaker's suprasegmentals and non-verbal characteristics. To help the student locate an appropriate model, the instructor may provide a list of possible speakers and segments as well as describe the characteristics of ineffective models (too fast, little pausing, monotonic speech, etc.). In addition, since students have had the opportunity to identify their own challenges using a diagnostic pronunciation test, their instructor might assist them in choosing a model that will be most beneficial for remedying their challenges.

3. **Segment Purpose and Tone.** Once their model speaker has been approved by the instructor, students select a speech segment and analyze it in terms of speaker stance and purpose (persuasion, providing information, and/or entertainment), speech characteristics (e.g., volume, rate, pausing, and intonation) and non-verbal communication (e.g., facial expressions, gestures, use of space). They also pay attention to whether any of these areas change during the segment and try to understand why.

For example, a model speaker may speak loudly with less pitch variation in a part of the segment when they communicate anger.

4. **Speech/Non-Verbal Analysis.** Once they have a transcript of the segment (either via the Internet or through transcribing it themselves), students analyze the speech for whatever features of pronunciation they need to focus on. For instance, a student who tends to speak with little pausing and a monotone voice may make notes on the model's use of pausing and prominence. In addition, students note the model speaker's facial expressions and gestures (particularly ones that coincide with stress or intonation patterns) and write this information on the transcript after the word or phrase that accompanies the non-verbal movement. After they have completed their transcription with notes, their instructor provides guidance on accuracy.

Having completed the *Analysis* phase, the students move on to the phase called *Mirroring*, in which they try to imitate their model speaker's delivery of the selected speech segment. Their aim in imitation is to internalize their model speaker's voice (as described in Chapter 4), including their pronunciation of segments, prosodics in synchrony with their non-verbal communication patterns, and pragmatic expressions in expressing their communicative purpose, stance, and emotion. In imitating this voice, the learners are striving to "be" their model speaker in the same way that children often pretend in play at "being" other people. The *Mirroring* phase has five steps: the students start and stop the video as they mirror each thought group; they produce the segment using the "Read, Look Up, and Say" technique with a partner; they produce it using the "Read, Look-Up, and Say" technique with an audience while being video-recorded; they analyze their video for pronunciation, non-verbal communication, and faithfulness of the mirroring; and finally they give their presentation from memory, producing a final video in front of an audience, later evaluating their video and setting goals for the future.

5. **Mirror Model.** Once students have analyzed their short segment, they focus on putting each thought group into their short-term memory. They access the original video and click "pause" after each thought group or sentence. They then say that phrase or sentence immediately after the video, focusing on mirroring the exact words and imitating the body language of the original speaker. If desired, they can first mirror the spoken language and then add the body language. They should make eye contact with

the original speaker and say each phrase while looking at the original speaker.

6. **Internalizing Speech Practice Activity.** Up to this point, students have familiarized themselves with the original speaker, but it is now time to internalize the speaker's voice so as to make it their own. They do this by using their marked transcript and reading each thought group, looking up, and saying it to a partner. It is crucial to remind students that they need to look up and speak the thought group to their audience, as some students have the tendency to just read the transcript without looking up. Doing it without looking up cuts off connection with the audience and does not allow sufficient time for adequately long enough pauses to be inserted between thought groups. The audience may consist of one other person or a group of listeners, but the key is that there must be a real audience for this step.

7. **Trial Version.** Students practice saying their transcript by reading each thought group, looking up, and saying it to an audience (other members of the class, as well as their instructor) who is listening for the first time as in any real communicative event. Students are video-recorded (they can practice a few times beforehand if they wish), and afterward their audience gives them feedback on how well they did.

8. **Trial Version Analysis.** Students view the trial version produced in Step 7 and complete a self-critique in which they identify strengths and challenges of their performance so far. Using a top-down approach, they analyze suprasegmentals, such as use of prominence, intonation (including pitch range), non-verbal communication, such as gesture, eye contact, and proxemics, and how effectively they are mirroring the stance, emotions, and tone of the model speaker.

9. **Final Version/Final Version Analysis.** Once again, students perform their segment in front of a small audience, usually other members of the class and the instructor, without reading the transcript. They try to focus on expressing the emotion and stance of the model speaker as well as improving their performance in one or two areas which they have identified as less successful in their trial version. If they make a mistake or forget a word or phrase, they can just ad lib. They may record several times until they are satisfied with their performance. After recording, students will complete a self-critique of their final version, focusing on what

they have improved from their trial version. In addition, they will note down strategies for continued improvement in those identified areas as they reflect on future performance in planned or extemporaneous speech.

The third phase of the MP is *Channeling*, the purpose of which is to transfer to another communicative situation the voice they have internalized during the MP, this voice being a holistic synchronized composite of pronunciation, non-verbals, and pragmatic patterns expressing a particular identity, stance, and emotional tone.

10. **Channeling & Evaluation.** Channeling involves asking students to apply what they have learned, as they deliver (in front of an audience) original content that is their own, such as a previously recorded talk, a self-introduction, a written speech, etc., using the voice of their model speaker – communicating their own material the way they think their model would have said it using verbal and non-verbal aspects of their model's speech. This is an attempt to apply, or carry over, the learned pronunciation features to deliver the students' own content, demonstrating the transferability of "controlled" patterns learned in the MP to "free" speech activities. After channeling, students will again complete a self-critique, comparing their channeling performance – if possible – to the diagnostic speech sample from Step 1. Students will benefit from seeing the progress they have made over the course of the project, and this is an excellent opportunity for students to reflect on how well they have achieved their unique goals. Students may also reflect on strategies for continued improvement in any areas that they still identify as challenges.

Where to Find Videos of Speakers for Mirroring Projects

It is important, when executing the MP, to provide students with access to a good source of video-recorded speakers talking to live or video audiences. Students may choose any video-recorded example – for example, a monologue or dialogue from television, film, or theater, an advertisement, or a public service announcement, to name a few other video-based options. However, TED Talks have been a popular choice among students for at least three reasons:

1. TED Talks are readily available excellent models. Presenters convey information they care about confidently and with feeling,

and they engage and connect with their live audiences. Students who are working on improving their delivery, the liveliness of their speech, the way they use gesture or command their physical space, etc., seem to gravitate towards such models.

2. TED Talks are posted online with transcripts. The transcript for any given TED Talk is very accessible and usually broken up into thought groups or short phrases; when students are working with a TED Talk transcript, they can click on a given thought group over and over again to listen to a particular pronunciation feature or watch non-verbal expressions in that particular part of the video. Another important feature of these videos is that the speech rate can be slowed down to 75% or even 50% of the original speed. Such adjustments can prove helpful for L2 learners in identifying which word or syllable receives stress or precisely which word is being highlighted through body language.

3. These speeches are often informative, funny, and/or persuasive. So, in addition to working on the pronunciation features that they want to improve, students can also work on the pragmatics of communicating in English (e.g., pausing for dramatic effect before delivering the punchline of a story or joke).

Case Studies

To demonstrate in detail the way the MP works with individual students, the following section includes two case studies of ITAs working on different challenges related to delivery who undertook the MP in 2017. The first student is "Kan-Ting" (pseudonym), who is from Taiwan and speaks Mandarin and Taiwanese. The second student is "Manish" (pseudonym), who hails from India and speaks Tamil and Indian English. We include two case studies to illustrate the success of the MP with different types of students whom instructors may find in their classrooms. Kan-Ting has challenges with non-verbals (e.g., gesture, facial expression) and suprasegmentals (e.g., word stress, lack of prominence, and compressed pitch range), whereas Manish has challenges with word stress based on varietal differences in World Englishes and temporal measures of fluency (i.e., syllable rate, articulation rate, and mean length of runs). In both cases, we will focus primarily on these learners' improvement in two major areas: non-verbal communication and suprasegmental use.

Kan-Ting (Mandarin/Taiwanese NS)

Kan-Ting was an international graduate student enrolled in a course for ITAs at a large Midwestern university in the United States. He was majoring in biomedical engineering and was concurrently employed as a teaching assistant in a lab in his department. As such, he was in the process of building a new professional identity as a biomedical engineer. Kan-Ting's performance in developing a voice that communicates that identity will be analyzed over three points in time: Time 1 – an initial (diagnostic) recording, Time 2 – a mirroring recording, and Time 3 – a channeling recording.

Time 1: Initial Recording

An initial recording at Time 1 serves as a diagnostic for Kan-Ting. This was an opportunity for him to learn what he already did well and what areas in pronunciation (i.e., intelligibility) and delivery (i.e., impression management) he might work on for the duration of the MP. In this first recording, Kan-Ting presented his first micro-teaching presentation. A micro-teaching, as the name suggests, is a short presentation of content from his field, biomedical engineering, and is therefore a very authentic example of material that he, as a graduate teaching assistant, will need to teach with authority to his students. Figure 6.1 depicts a screenshot taken from the 30.9 second micro-teaching segment; it shows Kan-Ting standing in front of a white board on which he has written the title of the course, his name (edited to appear as his pseudonym), the title of the lab, and his agenda for his mock lab presentation.

In Transcript 6.1 below, showing what Kan-Ting says in the short clip, the following symbols and transcription conventions are used:

/ = short pause (less than 1.0 second in length)
// = long pause (greater than 1.0 second in length)
CAPS = prominence (marked by loudness and pitch change)
Underlining = peak stress, the syllable that receives the most stress in
a thought group
↗ = Rising Tone
→ = Level Tone (flat or a slight rise)
↘↗ = Fall-Rise pattern
↗↘ = Rise-Fall pattern
(( )) = visible conduct described inside double parentheses in italic font
[ ] = transcriber notes appear in brackets

TRANSCRIPT 6.1. Time 1 Micro-Teaching Kan-Ting

ok so the topic the topic of Lab 1 ((*timer is making sound, which interferes with his beginning; points to white board*)) the ↗↘TOPIC of lab one ((*points to board*)) / is ↗↘ERROR [sounds like ARROW] ((*points with left hand*)) ESTIMATION ((*points with left hand*)) / which is a pretty ↗↘SIMPLE lab ((*moves left hand*)) / but it's also very important ((*moves left hand down*)) / because / all ↘↗MEASUREMENTS ((*left hand; then switches paper*)) we ↗↘MADE ((*right hand moves down*)) / have its corresponding ((*moves hand down*)) errors // ↘↗SO ((*right hand moves down*)) / to have / to have an ↗↘IDEA ((*left hand moves down*)) / about ((*left hand moves down*)) / how ↗↘CLOSE ((*right hand moves down*)) your result ((*right hand moves down*)) ↘↗IS ((*right hand moves down*)) to the ↗↘TRUE ((*right hand moves down*)) value / you have ((*moves right hand down*)) to make an ↗↘ERROR [sounds like ARROW] estimation ((*points to board with left hand*))

FIGURE 6.1. Time 1 Recording of Kan-Ting

In this micro-teaching segment, we observe that Kan-Ting is already doing some things well. In this first speech paragraph, for example, Kan-Ting uses some body language in synchrony with his words to improve intelligibility. In this segment, he moves his left hand as he says the word *lab*. This same gesture is shown in the screenshot displayed in Figure 6.1 as he says the phrase *which is a pretty simple lab*. In addition, he tries to make eye contact with the audience in the room. Another positive aspect of this micro-teaching segment is that Kan-Ting uses some pausing, as is indicated by the slash marks, and he assigns prominence to the words *topic, error, estimation,* and *simple*.

While there are a few notable things that Kan-Ting does well, we are also able to identify some challenges as areas for improvement. In terms of non-verbals, Kan-Ting is quite limited in this first recording. He regularly uses a falling hand motion which begins waist-high and drops down. In this, his body language appears to mirror his overall lack of pitch change. See Figure 6.2 for the type of hand gesture which he uses on the word *errors* in the phrase, *have its corresponding errors.* Although he uses both his right hand and his left hand, he repeats the same type of gesture each time, switching his paper from one hand to the next as he repeatedly makes the downwards chop with his other. This pattern does not draw listeners' attention to key words.

FIGURE 6.2. Time 1 Recording of Kan-Ting with Limited Non-Verbals

The second challenge is word stress on certain key words: *also, important, corresponding,* and *errors.* The word *important* seems to be missing the first syllable *im* and the second syllable of this word does not have enough pitch change to indicate that he is giving it stress. The word *corresponding* is missing a pitch jump on the secondarily stressed syllable *cor.* This lack of pitch change for word stress further interferes with intelligibility because there is a lack of prominence on two important thought groups in this section: *but it's also very important* and in the phrase, *have its corresponding errors.* We cannot hear any changes in pitch, intensity, or length for the words *also* and *important*; these should be assigned more prominence based on the context of the lab overview. The key word *error* is a special case. The first time Kan-Ting says the word, he stresses it and points to it on the board as part of the phrase *error estimation*, making the word clear in that context. However, later on in the phrase *have its corresponding errors*, neither *corresponding* nor *errors* is clear. In fact, his voice trails off, making it hard to even decipher what the phrase is, so that the word *error* sounds something like *arrow*.

Additionally, in the phrase *but it's also very important*, we cannot hear any changes in pitch, intensity, or length for the words *also* and *important*; these should be assigned more prominence based on the context of the lab overview.

To further illustrate Kan-Ting's challenges in suprasegmentals, we would like to focus on his second speech paragraph in which, after his introduction, Kan-Ting goes over his agenda for the micro-teaching lesson, which is also written on the white board. Some features of his non-verbals work well. To improve his intelligibility, he points to many of the words on the board as he says them; for example, in Figure 6.3, he is pointing to the phrase *errors in measurements* as he reads it off. Here, too, we see Kan-Ting using effective pausing, especially between sentences and major thought groups. See Transcript 6.2, showing speech paragraph two below:

TRANSCRIPT 6.2. Speech Paragraph 2 Kan-Ting

> ok so ➜FIRST *((points to board))* ➚➘THIS is today's agenda // first we will talk about ➘➚ERRORS in ➚➘MEASUREMENTS *((points to words* errors *and* measurements *as he says them))* there are ➜two major kinds of errors in measurements // one is ➚➘SYSTEMATI [omits final consonant sound] error *((points to word* systematic*))* and the other one is ➚➘RANDOM error *((points to word* random*))* ➚➘NEXT / we will talk about ➜SKILLS / for error ➚➘ESTIMATION *((points to words* error estimation*))* // espec / especially as ➚ONE *((points to word* one*))* / measurement is ➜MADE *((points to board))* / or if only / or if ➜repeate [omits final consonant sound] *((points to board))* measurements are ➚➘MADE *((points as he says* repeated, measurements, *and* made*))* // then we will have some examples / and practice // so finally we will have a summary *((points to word* summary *on board))*

However, when listening to what he says, we find that, in this paragraph at Time 1, the words *systematic* and *repeated* are missing the final consonant sounds. The word *repeated*, in particular, is basically unintelligible; we had to listen to it several times before being able to identify it by looking at the white board, without which we would not have been able to understand. Some of his transition words, such as *then* and *finally*, need to be made more prominent by means of vowel length and pitch change, a commonly observed problem in NNS speech (cf. Pickering, 2001, reviewed in Chapter 3).

FIGURE 6.3. Time 1 Recording of Kan-Ting, Speech Paragraph 2

To illustrate Kan-Ting's lack of prominence assigned to transitions and key words, we use Praat (Boersma & Weenink, n.d.) to illustrate how flat the transition adverb *finally* and the key word *summary* are. Pitch was analyzed by first selecting the last thought group of the speech paragraph *so finally we will have a summary*. As a reminder, the top part of the screen represents vowel length and intensity and the bottom line shows pitch patterns. Using Praat acoustic analysis software, pitch contours were displayed below the spectrogram (see Figure 6.4) and pitch range was calculated using the 0.1 and 0.9 quantiles of the minimum and maximum pitch for this particular speech segment. We used these quantile values of pitch instead of the absolute minimum and maximum values because this allows us to effectively exclude a low level of background noise and thus allow us to measure changes in pitch range over time with more confidence (Boersma, personal communication to Meyers, July 27, 2021). The pitch range was calculated by subtracting the minimum (0.1 quantile value) from the maximum (0.9 quantile value) numbers, and these values are reported in Table 6.2. (Note: All subsequent minimum and maximum Praat values in this chapter are reported in quantiles.) As shown here, the thought group itself is not transcribed as having any prominence; there are not any words in CAPS. When we perform a Praat analysis, we do not perceive any pitch changes on either of the two words *finally* and *summary*, and we see that the pitch range between minimum and maximum values is extremely flat and narrow – a mere 20 Hz – which is not enough to clearly perceive these two important words.

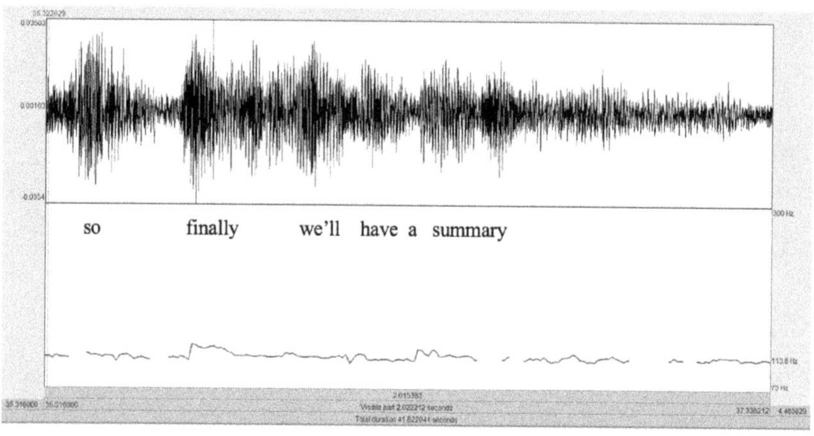

FIGURE 6.4. Praat Analysis of Kan-Ting, Time 1, Speech Paragraph 2

TABLE 6.2. Pitch Characteristics of Kan-Ting Time 1, Speech Paragraph 2

Minimum Pitch	Maximum Pitch	Pitch Range
110.7 Hz	130.7 Hz	20.0 Hz

A common important form of prominence in speech is the use of contrastive stress to compare and contrast terms; we see this in speech paragraph two. In his class overview, Kan-Ting contrasts the words *systematic* and *random*, as well as the words *one* versus *repeated*. An effective speaker would place extra high[1] pitch and vowel length on those words in this context. However, Kan-Ting does not place prominence on any of these words in this context; his pitch range throughout is only 21.3 Hz, very flat and monotonal. See Table 6.3 and the provided excerpt from Transcript 6.2 for evidence of this:

TABLE 6.3. Pitch Characteristics of Kan-Ting Time 1, Speech Paragraph 2: Comparison and Contrast

> one is ↗↘SYSTEMATI [omits final consonant sound] error ((*points to word* systematic)) and the other one is the ↗↘RANDOM error ((*points to word* random))

Minimum Pitch	Maximum Pitch	Pitch Range
105.7 Hz	127.0 Hz	21.3 Hz

In Chapter 3, we reported Pickering's (2001) findings that speech paragraphs for NNSs are not the same as those of NSs. Yuan and Liberman (2014, p. 67) observe that, for NSs of many languages, "[i]t has been observed in many languages that the pitch contour over the course of an utterance has a downward trend, normally called F0 declination in the literature" (e.g., Cohen, Collier, & 't Hart, 1982; Ladd, 1984). (F0, or fundamental frequency, is the lowest partial of a periodic sound wave, which our brains interpret as pitch.) They go on to say:

> In our English data, the baseline and top line are similar, both consisting of three parts: initial plateau, middle declination, and final lowering. In Mandarin Chinese, the top line is similar to the top line in English, while the baseline is close to a straight line. (Yuan & Liberman, 2014, p. 72)

We see a prime example of Kan-Ting's overall narrow flat intonation in speech paragraph two of his speech, which has no clear declination from high key to low key as the paragraph progresses. In the previous two tables (6.2 and 6.3), we see that segments of Kan-Ting's speech have very little F0 variation, if any. If we listen to the whole speech paragraph, we observe that Kan-Ting's speech does not have much declination over the course of the entire paragraph. See Table 6.4 which illustrates the narrowness of the pitch range over this entire speech paragraph:

TABLE 6.4. F0 Declination over Kan-Ting Time 1, Speech Paragraph 2

Minimum Pitch	Maximum Pitch	Pitch Range
109.3 Hz	137.8 Hz	28.5 Hz

To summarize, an analysis of Kan-Ting's Time 1 diagnostic recording establishes that his major focus in improving his intelligibility should be to work on pitch change for placing stress on important words, but more importantly, for indicating what words he wants the listener to perceive as prominent, and to use key (high pitch and low pitch) with a wider pitch range for drawing the listener's attention to the beginnings and endings of utterances and speech paragraphs.

Model Speaker: Anthony Atala

In selecting a speech model, Kan-Ting chose a segment from a 2011 TED Talk by Anthony Atala, a researcher in regenerative medicine, entitled "Printing a Human Kidney" (Atala, 2011).[2] In this segment, Atala (a NNS of English himself who also speaks French, Italian, and Spanish), explains how to grow stem cells outside the body. He is an excellent communicator in his use of appropriate pausing and his highlighting of prominent words through pitch changes and gesture; these features make him a very suitable model for Kan-Ting.

Atala uses gestures to highlight the words which he emphasizes in this part of the talk; for instance, he uses his left hand (palm upward) to highlight the words *organ, scaffold,* and *biomaterial.* A salient example of this occurs at 4:29 in the video when Atala uses a palm upward gesture for the word *organ* as he says the phrase *If you do have a diseased or injured organ...* In addition, he often employs iconic gestures that are closely related to the semantic content of his speech. For instance, at 4:31 of the video, he uses his thumb and forefinger together to illustrate the phrase *very small piece.* To illustrate the word *shape,* at 4:46 in the video, he uses both hands and forms a ball-like structure to demonstrate the idea of shaping something.

In Transcript 6.3, we include our own original transcription of the segment that Kan-Ting chose to mirror from Atala's speech. In our transcript, we use the same conventions indicated previously in this chapter (page 101) to characterize suprasegmentals, and we have added our own commentary to vividly portray his non-verbal communication throughout this speech segment.

TRANSCRIPT 6.3. Model Speech Segment from Atala (Time Signatures 4:25 – 4:52)

> so the concept here ((*opens hands*)) // so if you DO ((*fingers of right hand move outward*)) have a ↗↘DISEASED or injured ↗↘ORGAN ((*opens palm of left hand*)) / we take a ↗↘VERY SMALL PIECE ((*fingers together*)) of that tissue / less than ↗↘HALF ((*points*)) the size of a ↗↘POSTAGE STAMP // we then tease the cells →APART / we grow the cells outside the →BODY // we then take a ↗↘SCAFFOLD ((*palm up*)) / a ↗↘BIOMATERIAL ((*palm up*)) / ↗↘AGAIN ((*right hand moves forward*)) looks very much like a piece of your ↘↗BLOUSE / or your ↗↘SHIRT / we then ↗↘SHAPE ((*hands form a shape*)) that material / and we then use those cells to ↗↘COAT ((*right hand coating imaginary material*)) / that material / one ↗↘LAYER ((*moves hand*)) at a time //

Atala's pitch clearly rises on key words like *organ, half,* and *shape,* making them stand out as important to the message he is trying to convey. In addition, his pitch rises and falls across a wide range – from a minimum pitch of 123.5 Hz to a maximum of 203.8 Hz for a range of 80.3 Hz. Table 6.5 shows the pitch range of these suprasegmental patterns in Atala's speech.

TABLE 6.5. Pitch Characteristics of Anthony Atala TED Talk

Minimum Pitch	Maximum Pitch	Pitch Range
123.5 Hz	203.8 Hz	80.3 Hz

Clearly, Atala is a great model for Kan-Ting not only in terms of the content of his talk (as it relates to his major in bioengineering, and his concurrent employment as a biomedical engineering teaching assistant), but also in terms of his use of suprasegmentals and body language.

Time 2: Kan-Ting Mirroring Anthony Atala

At Time 2, a video-recording was made of Kan-Ting mirroring Anthony Atala. Remember that the mirroring task asks students to imitate everything they can about their model, including non-verbals and communication of stance and emotion; in other words, to try to "be" that person. The length of Kan-Ting's mirroring segment is short, about 30–45 seconds. Even though students can practice with a script, the final version of the Time 2 presentation should be memorized. The audience consists of the instructor, two peers (international graduate students), and a NS undergraduate teaching assistant. Transcript 6.4 shows Kan-Ting's mirroring of Atala's TED Talk.

TRANSCRIPT 6.4. Kan-Ting Time 2

> so the concept ↗↘HERE ((*moves right hand*)) // so if you DO have a ↗↘DISEASED ((*right hand with palm up*)) or injured ↗↘ORGAN ((*moves left hand and opens palm*)) / we take a ↗↘VERY SMALL PIECE ((*fingers of right hand together*)) / of that tissue ((*moves hand*)) / less than ↗↘HALF the size of a ↗↘POSTAGE STAMP ((*moves right hand in two rhythmic beats*)) // we then tease the cells →APART ((*moves right hand up and away with palm open*)) / we grow the cells outside the →BODY ((*hands apart*)) // we then take a ↗↘SCAFFOLD ((*palm up shoulder height; eyebrows raised*)) / a ↗↘BIOMATERIAL ((*moves hand with palm up*)) / ↗↘AGAIN / looks very much like a piece of your ↘↗BLOUSE ((*fist hand gesture*)) / or your ↗↘SHIRT ((*fist hand gesture*)) // we then ↗↘SHAPE ((*hands closed forming a shape; eyebrow movement*)) the material / and we then use those cells to ↗↘COAT ((*right hand coating imaginary material*)) the material / one ↗↘LAYER ((*moves hand continuing to coat imaginary material*)) at a time //

If we pay close attention to Kan-Ting's body language and the words which he makes prominent, we see that his gestures here at Time 2 are much more varied than those at Time 1, and they occur more in sync with the words which he's highlighting: *here, organ, shape,* and *coat.*

Interestingly, Kan-Ting is not only synchronizing his gestures with those words, but some of his gestures are exactly the same as Atala's were in the original recording for words like *piece, postage stamp, scaffold,* and *shape,* among others. Kan-Ting even uses Atala's eyebrow movements on the words *scaffold* and *shape.* These aspects of his recording contribute to the visual and auditory impression that Kan-Ting is striving to "be" Atala, internalizing his voice. Figures 6.5 and 6.6 show Kan-Ting's non-verbals for the phrase *diseased or injured organ.* We can see that he first (Figure 6.5) gestures with his right hand to highlight *diseased* and then subsequently (Figure 6.6) raises his left hand for *injured organ,* visibly demonstrating two distinct types.

FIGURES 6.5 & 6.6. Kan-Ting Gesturing with *diseased or injured organ*

Pitch ranges for this part indicate that Kan-Ting's pitch variation has improved a great deal compared to Time 1 (shown in Transcript 6.2 on page 104). Table 6.6 and the provided excerpt from Transcript 6.4 illustrate that for this section of the transcript at Time 2, Kan-Ting's pitch varies from a minimum of 118.6 Hz to a maximum of 270.2 Hz, with a markedly wider range of 151.6 Hz.

TABLE 6.6. Pitch Characteristics of Kan-Ting Time 2

> so the concept ⬈⬊HERE ((*moves right hand*)) //
> so if you DO have a ⬈⬊DISEASED ((*right hand with palm up*))
> or injured ⬈⬊ORGAN ((*moves left hand and opens palm*))

Minimum Pitch	Maximum Pitch	Pitch Range
118.6 Hz	270.2 Hz	151.6 Hz

Just as Atala did, Kan-Ting now uses more iconic gestures to emphasize certain key words. For instance, Figure 6.7 shows Kan-Ting forming his hands into almost the same iconic gesture to indicate *shape* that Atala used in the original recording.

FIGURE 6.7. Recording of Kan-Ting Time 2 *we then shape the material*

Finally, Figure 6.8 shows Kan-Ting spreading his arms outwardly to refer to cells that are outside rather than inside the body. It is interesting that this gesture is actually Kan-Ting's own creation, not a mirroring of Atala; nevertheless, it is certainly the sort of gesture Atala might have used, and one that serves to make the content clearer. Overall, in his recording at Time 2, Kan-Ting actually seems to use more body language than Atala. This increase in body language from Time 1 to Time 2 does not seem artificial or misplaced.

FIGURE 6.8. Recording of Kan-Ting Time 2 *The cells are outside the body.*

In mirroring Atala at Time 2, Kan-Ting does an excellent job of lengthening vowels in stressed syllables in the following words marked as prominent in Transcript 6.4 on page 109: *here, do, organ, postage stamp, outside, scaffold, biomaterial, shape,* and *coat*. In terms of pitch change, words that particularly stand out are: *here, do, organ, piece, postage stamp, scaffold,* and *shape*. If we analyze Time 2 in terms of pitch range, we see that it goes from 114.6 Hz up to 269.5 Hz, which is a much wider range of 154.9 Hz! Thus, based on both non-verbal communication and verbal components of his performance, we can observe that Kan-Ting has – in many ways – succeeded in "being" Atala in this re-performance of the TED Talk, not only dramatically changing the suprasegmental features of his speech but also his use of non-verbal communication.

Time 3: Kan-Ting Channeling Atala

The final stage of the MP is *channeling*, in which the task is for the student to imagine that they are the person that they mirrored while they are producing their own original content. What Kan-Ting does here is to try to use Atala's voice to re-record his previous micro-teaching segment delivering a lecture for a mock biomedical engineering lab. The length of the segment is short, only about one to two minutes. The audience is the same as that for mirroring (i.e., the instructor, two ITA peers, and one undergraduate teaching assistant), and once again the performance is video-recorded. Similar to Time 2, ITAs are allowed the opportunity to re-record several times if they want to do so. The channeled segment is presented in Transcript 6.5. Several words are marked as prominent: *diseased, heart, cardiac, out, indicator, identify,* and *status.* Even in his over-view of the mock lab, he marks new information as prominent: *principles, procedure,* and *examples.*

TRANSCRIPT 6.5. Kang-Ting Channeling Atala: Mock Biomedical Engineering Lab

↗↘SO ((*left arm downward*)) / if you do have a ↗↘DISEASED ((*moves fist to right*)) / or injured ↗↘HEART ((*moves fist to left*)) / then your ↗↘CARDIA [omits final consonant sound] output may be ↗↘OUT ((*moves right hand way off to the right*)) of this range // so / ((*left fist*)) it's a very useful ↗↘INDICATOR ((*left fist upward*)) / for physicians to ↗↘IDENTIFY ((*right hand open*)) / the ↗↘STATUS of a ↗↘HEART ((*closed fist downward*)) //

OK / so in ↗↘TODAY'S class ((*fist downward*)) / ↗↘FIRST ((*right thumb outward*)) / we're gonna talk about the ↗↘PRINCIPLES ((*right thumb outward*)) / of the ↗↘DYE DILUTION ((*right thumb outward*)) // and ↗↘NEXT ((*right thumb outward*)) / we'll go through the ↗↘PROCEDURES ((*left hand outward*)) of ↗↘DYE DILUTION ((*left hand outward*)) // and ↗↘FINALLY ((*right fist*)) / if we have →TIME ((*right fist*)) / we'll do some ↗↘EXAMPLES ((*both hands facing forward and away from his body*)) of dye dilution //

Two screen shots (Figures 6.9 and 6.10) from this video-recording illustrate Kan-Ting's use of body language, borrowed from Atala, which Kan-Ting channels for use with the transition word *first* (shown in Figure 6.9) and a word providing new information, *examples* (shown in Figure 6.10).

Turning to Kan-Ting's use of suprasegmentals, we can hear that in his first speech paragraph, he makes the following words prominent: *diseased, cardiac, indicator, identify, status,* and *heart.* Equally impressive is Kan-Ting's wider pitch range as shown in Table 6.7 with the provided excerpt from Transcript 6.5, to highlight the transition words and new information in his overview of his lesson for that day.

FIGURES 6.9 & 6.10. Kan-Ting Channeling Atala: Gestures for *first* and *examples*

TABLE 6.7. Kan-Ting Channeling Atala: Prosodics Signal Transition Words and New Information

OK / so in ↗↘TODAY'S class ((*left fist moves downward*)) /
↗↘FIRST ((*right thumb outward*)) /
we're gonna talk about the ↗↘PRINCIPLES ((*right thumb outward*)) /
of the ↗↘DYE DILUTION ((*right thumb outward*)) //

Minimum Pitch	Maximum Pitch	Pitch Range
102.5 Hz	236.7 Hz	134.2 Hz

In this part of his Time 3 mock lab, we hear clear prominence on the words *today's*, *first*, *principles*, and *dye dilution*. Table 6.7 shows a clear increase in pitch range for a total of 134.2 Hz.

Observable Changes From Time 1 to Time 3

In this section, we summarize Kan-Ting's improvement over the three time periods and focus mainly on the changes in his non-verbal communication and his overall increase in pitch range to indicate prominence and declination (gradual descent in pitch) over speech paragraphs.

Non-Verbal Communication

Table 6.8 summarizes the changes in Kan-Ting's non-verbal communication from Time 1 (original micro-teaching) to Time 2 (mirroring) and Time 3 (channeling). These changes serve to make his speech more intelligible and more interesting to his audience.

TABLE 6.8. Kan-Ting's Non-Verbal Communication at Times 1, 2, and 3

Time 1	Time 2	Time 3
Sometimes faces audience. Points to board.	Faces audience. Looks back and forth.	Faces audience. Looks back and forth.
Does not smile. Little eye contact and lack of body orientation towards audience.	Audience orientation through: smiling, eye contact, and body orientation towards audience.	Audience orientation through: smiling, eye contact, and body orientation towards audience.
Hands are waist height. Hand moves down on last word in thought group (*estimation*, *lab*, etc.).	Hands are shoulder height. Uses both hands in various directions.	Hands are higher up on body. Uses both hands in various directions.
	Uses more varied and iconic gestures, e.g., *shape*, *one layer*, and *coats*.	Uses more varied gestures, e.g., finger for *first*, both hands out for *examples*.
	Emphasizes new information, e.g., *shape* (the material).	Emphasizes new information, e.g., *identify*, *principles*.
	Uses motor gestures (with fist) to show rhythmic beats.	

Table 6.8 shows that while Kan-Ting's non-verbal communication was quite limited during his initial recording, Time 2 and Time 3 include much more varied body language, including iconic gestures, such as for the word *shape*. In Times 2 and 3, he moves his hands higher up relative

to his body rather than moving them waist high downward, contributing to the impression that his pitch is no longer flat for prominent words. Recall from Time 1 that Kan-Ting did not use much pitch variation for prominence and that at times, even though his hand movement downward might have been intended to indicate emphasis, it did not draw the audience's attention as his pitch remained rather flat. At Time 1, Kan-Ting used the white board extensively to portray the structure of his mock lab. However, at Times 2 and 3, he uses only his body language (gestures, facial expressions, and eyebrow movements) to highlight the rhetorical structure of that mock lab. At Time 1, he compensated for his lack of clear prominence through visual aids; however, by Times 2 and 3, he is using his voice and non-verbal communication to communicate prominence.

Suprasegmentals

In addition to his improvement with non-verbal communication, Kan-Ting also makes gains in his use of suprasegmentals. Table 6.9 summarizes the increase in pitch range from Time 1 to Time 3. To illustrate how this affects prominence in his speech, we compare two similar sentences from Time 1 and Time 3 (see Figures 6.11 and 6.12). Although they are not exactly the same words, these two introductions to mock labs are similar in their purpose and intent for the speaker and in terms of their organization, not only in terms of the language used but also in terms of use of key to indicate speech paragraphs.

TABLE 6.9. Comparison of Kan-Ting's Pitch Range Times 1, 2, and 3

Time	Time 1 (Micro-Teaching 1)	Time 2 (Mirroring Project)	Time 3 (Channeling)
Pitch Min.; Max.	109.3 Hz; 137.8 Hz	114.6 Hz; 269.5 Hz	105.2 Hz; 260.0 Hz
Range	28.5 Hz	154.9 Hz	154.8 Hz

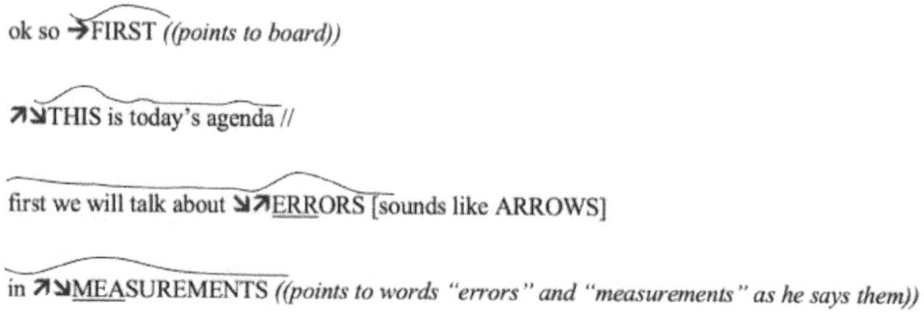

ok so →FIRST *((points to board))*

↗↘THIS is today's agenda //

first we will talk about ↘↗ERRORS [sounds like ARROWS]

in ↗↘MEASUREMENTS *((points to words "errors" and "measurements" as he says them))*

FIGURE 6.11. Pitch Contour Representation of Time 1 Kan-Ting

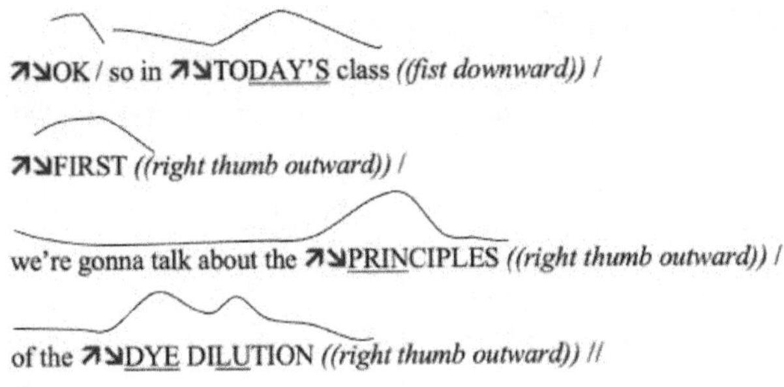

FIGURE 6.12. Pitch Contour Representation of Time 3 Kan-Ting

The two pitch contour representations in Figures 6.11 and 6.12 above show some important contrasts between Time 1 and Time 3. We see a general lack of prominence during Time 1, and we do not see much declination from the beginning of thought groups to the ends of thought groups. However, at Time 3, we observe much clearer prominence on important words that illustrate the rhetorical structure of his agenda for the day. Not only do the pitch contours illustrate improvement over the course of the MP, but we can also compare the increase in pitch range in the two comparison sentences. As can be seen in Table 6.10 below, Kan-Ting's overall pitch range in these two sentences increases by 80.1 Hz from Time 1 to Time 3.

TABLE 6.10. Comparison of Kan-Ting's Pitch Range between Excerpts from Time 1 and Time 3

Time	Minimum Pitch	Maximum Pitch	Pitch Range
Time 1	111.7 Hz	165.8 Hz	54.1 Hz
Time 3	102.5 Hz	236.7 Hz	134.2 Hz
Change	− 9.2 Hz	+ 70.9 Hz	+ 80.1 Hz

Thus, in the areas of suprasegmental pronunciation, as well as non-verbal communication, we can see documented evidence of the influence of the MP on this ITA's progress in mastering verbal and non-verbal features that improve his intelligibility by internalizing the voice of an effective model speaker. Kan-Ting exemplifies one type of student with challenges in non-verbal communication and suprasegmentals, specifically a lack of sufficient pitch range to communicate clear prominence and non-verbal communication to complement that prominence. In the next section, we will describe a student with a different set of needs.

Manish (Indian English/Tamil NS)

Manish was an ITA from India living and studying in the United States who spoke a variety of World English (Indian English) and whose native language was Tamil. Like Kan-Ting, Manish was an international graduate student enrolled in a course for ITAs at a large Midwestern university in the United States; however, his academic major was computer science and he was not yet employed as a teaching assistant in his department at the time of his class enrollment. (Recall that Kan-Ting's academic major was biomedical engineering, and he was concurrently teaching a lab.) As we did in describing Kan-Ting, Manish's performance will be analyzed at three points of time: Time 1 – an initial (diagnostic) recording, Time 2 – a mirroring recording, and Time 3 – a channeling recording.

Time 1: Initial Recording

An initial recording at Time 1 serves as a diagnostic for Manish to identify his strengths and weaknesses in pronunciation (i.e., intelligibility) and delivery (i.e., impression management). In this first recording, Manish presents his first micro-teaching presentation from his field, computer science. Figure 6.13 presents a screenshot taken from a sixteen-second micro-teaching segment; it shows Manish standing in front of a white board on which he has written the topic of his micro-teaching: *Algorithm Analysis*. We also see his name (edited to appear as his pseudonym), the word *complexity*, with arrows to the words *time* and *space* (with a circle drawn around the word *time*), the words *Big Oh*, *Big Theta*, and *Big Omega* (with a circle drawn around the words *Big Oh*), and part of a visual on the right-hand side of the board. On the left, we see the word *How*, and underneath it he has written three points.

Transcript 6.6 shows what Manish says in the short clip. Refer to page 101 for an explanation of the transcription conventions used.

TRANSCRIPT 6.6. Time 1 Micro-Teaching Manish

> so we'll be discussing TODAY on / we'll be talking about ↗↘ALGORITHM ANALYSIS ((*points to words* algorithm *and* analysis)) / so um / when you see these two ↘↗[unintelligible; sounds like the word *stations*] ((*holds hands high and moves them slightly*)) / so uh what comes to your mind what do you ↘↗FEEL like uh what do you think about ↘↗ALGORITHM / so uh anything comes to your MIND ((*moves hands outward as he says* mind)) Lily do you have anything to say ↗↘about ↗it //

We are able to identify several strengths in Manish's spoken English and delivery of content. For instance, he has written some key terms on the board, and he is pointing to them as he says them while making eye contact with his audience (see Figure 6.13 below). Also, he is using interactive teaching skills by asking his audience to define the term *algorithm*. He even calls on one student in the audience, Lily (the undergraduate teaching assistant for his section), to define it for him. In terms of suprasegmentals, he is giving prominence to a few important words, such as *algorithm analysis*, *feel*, and *mind*. In Figure 6.14, we can see Manish holding his hands up and out as he puts prominence on the word *mind*.

FIGURE 6.13. Time 1 Recording of Manish with Use of White Board

FIGURE 6.14. Time 1 Recording of Manish Gesturing for Prominence on *mind*

Even though Manish is using some effective teaching skills and his grammar and vocabulary are relatively strong, we are able to identify several challenges in his use of suprasegmentals. The first challenge is word stress on some of his key terms: *algorithm* and *analysis.* Especially on the word *algorithm*, we do not hear much difference between each of the stressed syllables. Instead, each syllable appears to have equal weight in terms of length, pitch, and volume. Fortunately, because he has written these words on the board and is pointing to them, we can understand them.

Perhaps the bigger suprasegmental challenges for Manish relate to his use of pausing and overall rhythm. In the short segment (Time 1), Manish merely pauses a total of 2.1 seconds; his mean pause rate is 0.4 seconds! In addition, he produces several thought groups without pausing between them, as shown here in this line from Transcript 6.6:

> so uh what comes to your mind what do you ↘↗FEEL like uh what do you think about ↘↗ALGORITHM

A native speaker might pause after *mind, like,* and *algorithm* as these are the final words in three independent utterances.

As a way to identify Manish's use of pausing and speech rate (measures of fluency), we analyzed this partial segment from Time 1, in which Manish did not pause at all, as well as Manish's entire Time 1 Micro-Teaching segment (Transcript 6.6). Using Kang et al.'s (2010) framework, we analyzed both transcripts in terms of total number of syllables, total pause time, total articulation (speaking) time, articulation rate (minus pause time), and mean length of run (average number of syllables produced in utterances between pauses of 0.1 seconds and above). See Table 6.11 below for calculations for Time 1 during the shorter segment, as well as during the whole segment:

TABLE 6.11. Manish Time 1 Measures of Fluency

	Time 1 (partial segment)	Time 1 (whole segment)
Total syllables	22 syllables	73 syllables
Total pause time	0 seconds	2.1 seconds
Total articulation time	3.8 seconds	16.0 seconds
Articulation rate (minus pause time)	5.8 syllables	5.3 syllables
Mean length of run (syllables/runs)	**22 syllables** (22 syllables/1 run)	**12.2 syllables** (73 syllables/6 runs)

If we analyze the partial Transcript 6.6, we see that Manish takes 3.8 seconds to produce 22 syllables; this gives him an articulation rate of 5.8 syllables per second. If we include the whole segment, we find that he speaks for 16.0 seconds and that during that time he produces 73 syllables, giving him an articulation rate of 5.3 syllables per second and a mean length of run of 12.2 syllables. For best comprehensibility, the "ideal [articulation] rate for NS listeners of NNS speech is 4.1 compared to 4.7 for NS" (Kang et al., 2010, p. 555). Manish's articulation rate of 5.3 to 5.8 syllables is well above this threshold. When we consider his mean length of run for both the shorter segment and the longer one, we see that both contain quite a large number of syllables. So, Manish needs to slow his speech rate in order to become more intelligible to his U.S. audience.

Manish does give some prominence to focus words, but the words are not highlighted in the way that native speakers of U.S. American English would expect; research indicates that the vowels in prominent words should be four times as long as vowels in unstressed syllables (House, 1961). This is not the case for Manish. The vowels in words that he makes prominent are only slightly longer, nowhere near four times as long. Without pausing and additional vowel length, it is difficult to pick out the prominent words in Manish's speech.

To summarize, Manish needs to focus on incorporating longer pauses into his speech at thought group boundaries, give prominence to the focus word in each thought group by giving it far more length, and add more pitch variation to the stressed syllable in those focus words. In addition, using gestures to highlight those words could help.

Model Speaker: Steve Jobs

For his speech model, Manish chose a keynote address by Steve Jobs (2007)[3] in which he introduces the original iPhone at Macworld San Francisco. Because Manish is majoring in computer science, this is an appropriate choice in terms of speaking model and content. In addition, this segment has several unique characteristics which may have appealed to Manish. Steve Jobs incorporates very long pauses, he speaks in relatively short thought groups, he stresses important words through increased intensity, with extra vowel length and pitch changes, and, at the end, he repeats his three main points to make himself comprehensible to his audience and to leave a lasting impression.

Steve Jobs does not employ many gestures to highlight prominent words or ideas; instead, he mainly relies on visuals on a screen. He does, however, use a few iconic gestures, such as when he describes how fortunate one is to work on *just one of these* revolutionary technology products at minute 26:50 in the video. As Jobs faces the audience, he raises the index finger on his left hand upward to visibly illustrate *one*. Towards the end of this segment at 28:44, Jobs also uses his hands to highlight the syllable *break* on *breakthrough internet communications device*, extending his hands outward, away from his body. As he does this, the fingers on his left hand are extended, and his right hand is clasped around the device he is using to advance his slides. In the background, we observe the words *iPod*, *phone*, and *internet*, with illustrative visuals underneath each one, on the large screen.

Even though Jobs does not use many gestures or other types of body language to emphasize his points, he does make effective use of suprasegmentals for prominence. In our own original transcript that we provide of Job's talk (Transcript 6.7), the same conventions given previously in this chapter (page 101) are used to indicate suprasegmentals and non-verbal communication for this speech segment. Pause times are noted in brackets as transcriber notes to highlight how pauses are incorporated at strategic boundaries (i.e., thought groups) for effective delivery of his presentation.

TRANSCRIPT 6.7. Steve Jobs Introducing the iPhone at Macworld (Time Signatures 27:40 – 28:46)

> ↗↘TODAY / we're introducing / ↗↘THREE ((*3 fingers with left hand*)) ↗↘revolutionary ((*beat on* lu)) products of its class // [2.4 seconds of audience clapping] the ↗↘FIRST one // [2.7 seconds of pausing] is a ↗↘WIDE SCREEN / I-POD / ((*shows visual on screen*)) with ↗↘TOUCH CONTROLS // [10.3 seconds of audience clapping] the ↘↗SECOND // [1.7 seconds] is a ↗↘REVOLUTIONARY MOBILE PHONE // [9.0 seconds] and the ↗↘THIRD // [1.2 seconds] is a ↗↘BREAKTHROUGH INTERNET COMMUNICATION DEVICE // [4.4 seconds] ↗↘SO / [1.2 seconds] ((*opens hands*)) ↗↘three things / a WIDE screen I pod with →touch controls // [1.4 seconds] a REVOLUTIONARY mobile →phone // [4.0 seconds] and a ↗↘BREAKTHROUGH ((*opens hands on break*)) INternet ((*beat on in of internet*)) communications device

This transcript of Jobs' talk shows us that he pauses for a very long time (mainly while the audience claps for him, though applause would likely not occur in response to a teaching assistant!). More importantly, he speaks in relatively short thought groups of only on average 4.2 words; his longest thought group comprises nine words (some of which are compound words). In terms of prominence, Jobs makes certain key words stand out by giving them added intensity, extra vowel length, and extra pitch. Notice that the organizational words, such as *first, second,* and *third* are all made prominent, as are key/thematic noun phrases like *breakthrough internet communication device.* Also, it is interesting to note that the second time he repeats a phrase he still makes the first word prominent, e.g., *wide, revolutionary,* and *breakthrough.* Rules of prominence dictate that second mention should not be prominent, but in this case Jobs breaks those rules to remind his audience that these three products are indeed cutting edge by continuing to draw attention to words like *revolutionary* and *breakthrough.*

Thus, Steve Jobs is a very effective model for Manish based on his use of pausing and prominence to ensure that his audience pays attention and remembers the major characteristics of the new iPhone. In terms of non-verbal communication, his performance is not very animated, but he does make use of visuals on a large screen.

Time 2: *Manish Mirroring Steve Jobs*

At Time 2, a video recording is made of Manish mirroring Steve Jobs. Once again, the task requires students to try to communicate the same emotion and to try to "be" their model speaker. Transcript 6.8 below gives evidence of Manish mirroring Jobs for his project.

TRANSCRIPT 6.8. Manish Mirroring Steve Jobs

> ↗↘TODAY ((*hands folded chest high; extends right fingers*)) / we're introducing / ↗↘THREE ((*holds up three fingers*)) revolutionary ((*three fingers beat on lu*)) products ((*three fingers beat on pro*)) / of its CLASS ((*closes hand and smiles at audience*)) // [3.9 seconds of pausing] the ↗↘FIRST ((*hands folded chest height; moves fingers on right hand*)) one / is a WIDESCREEN ((*moves left hand down*)) / I-POD ((*moves left hand down*)) / with TOUCH CONTROLS ((*extends left hand towards imaginary visual on screen; smiles slightly*)) // [2.8 seconds] the ↗↘SECOND ((*moves both hands downward on sec; smiles slightly*)) // [1.1 seconds] is a ↗↘REVOLUTIONARY ((*moves both hands*)) MOBILE PHONE ((*moves left hand on mo and phone; smiles slightly*)) // [1.97 seconds] and the ↗↘THIRD ((*moves left hand downwards*)) / is a ↗↘BREAKTHROUGH ((*moves both hands downward on break*)) INTERNET ((*moves both hands slightly downward on in*)) COMMUNICATION ((*moves both hands slightly downward on ca*)) DEVICE

((moves both hands downward on vice; *smiles slightly)) // [2.8 seconds]
SO ((opens hands à la Steve Jobs)) / three things ((moves hands apart on
things)) // [2.3 seconds] a* ↘↗WIDE *((moves left hand downward with
pinky extended))* screen I pod with TOUCH controls *((smiles slightly)) //
[1.4 seconds] a* →REVOLUTIONARY *((moves left hand downward with
two fingers extended))* MOBILE PHONE *((smiles slightly)) // [1.4 seconds]
and a* ↗↘BREAKTHROUGH *((moves both hands downward))* INTERNET
COMMUNICATIONS DEVICE *((moves left hand slightly downward on syllable
stresses of* internet communications *and* device *and uses one more finger to
indicate the third thing))*

At Time 2, Manish uses substantially more body language in mirroring Steve Jobs than he does at Time 1 (and, interestingly, much more
body language than Jobs does). The main thing we observe is that Manish
keeps his hands at chest height, and he uses his hands (and occasionally
fingers) to highlight in three ways: to highlight the words that illustrate
the organization of the talk: *today, three, first, second,* and *third*; to highlight the words that he makes prominent, as when he mentions them for
the first time: *wide, iPod, touch controls, revolutionary,* and *breakthrough*;
and to indicate syllables in words that are no longer prominent – due
to the fact that they were previously mentioned – but whose stressed
syllables he nevertheless highlights through length: *mobile, internet, communications,* and *device.* Figure 6.15 illustrates highlighting the word *three*
by using his right hand and moving it downwards from chest height to
waist height. This is precisely the gesture that Steve Jobs uses in the
original recording.

FIGURE 6.15. Manish Time 2 Gesturing for *three*

Another place in which Manish uses gesture to mirror Steve Jobs is when he says the word *so*. Figure 6.16 below shows him, again, using exactly the same gesture as Steve Jobs does during his talk.

FIGURE 6.16. Manish Time 2 Gesturing for *so*

In total, the number of hand gestures which he incorporates in this short period of time is 25, compared to six for Steve Jobs. This might seem excessive, but the importance of this body language may be that it serves to help Manish lengthen vowels in stressed syllables, thus incorporating a more U.S. American English rhythm in his speech. No longer do all Manish's syllables receive equal length; instead, there is a clear pattern of lengthening or shortening of his syllables, giving him a more stress-timed rhythm. In terms of facial expressions, Manish smiles a total of seven times after he pauses and as he makes eye contact with his audience. Taking time to smile gives the impression that he is pleased to introduce the iPhone to his audience, and that he also wants to make a personal connection with audience members.

In terms of suprasegmentals, especially fluency, we see that at Time 2, Manish has made huge strides in his use of pausing, articulation rate, and mean length of runs. Table 6.12 below compares these temporal measures of fluency for Manish at Times 1 and 2:

TABLE 6.12. Manish Time 1 vs. Time 2 Measures of Fluency

	Time 1 (Diagnostic)	**Time 2 (Mirroring)**
Total syllables	73 syllables	97 syllables
Total pause time	2.1 seconds	19.8 seconds
Total articulation time	16.0 seconds	45.5 seconds
Articulation rate (minus pause time)	**5.3 syllables** (73 syllables/ 16.0 sec – 2.1 secs)	**3.8 syllables** (97 syllables/ 45.5 secs – 19.8 secs)
Mean length of run (syllables/runs)	**12.2 syllables** (73 syllables/6 runs)	**8.1 syllables** (97 syllables/12 runs)

Salient differences between Time 1 (diagnostic) and Time 2 (mirroring) include a dramatic increase in pause time from 2.1 seconds to 19.8 seconds, a decrease in articulation rate from 5.3 syllables to 3.8 syllables, and a decrease in mean length of run from 12.2 syllables to 8.1 syllables. These figures illustrate that Manish is pausing much longer, and he is producing roughly two-thirds the number of syllables per run as he did at Time 1. In mirroring Steve Jobs, Manish has incorporated and substantially added to the body language of Jobs, and he has successfully incorporated longer pauses between thought groups. Equally important is his lengthening of vowels in prominent words and stressed syllables through hand and finger gestures to improve intelligibility for his U.S. audience.

Time 3: Manish Channeling Steve Jobs

In the final stage of the MP, students channel their model speaker by imagining they are the person whom they mirrored while they are producing their own original content. In this case, Manish is being video-recorded as he takes his final exam for the course in which he was enrolled as an ITA. Instructions given to ITAs before their final exams are to try to channel their model speaker as they teach. The length of the segment is short; two of the audience members (the instructor and the undergraduate teaching assistant) are the same as that of Time 1, but there are two differences: the other ITA is not present and there is a new instructor present who is rating Manish as he does his micro-teaching. Due to the fact that this is a test, Manish is not allowed to re-record at any point during his micro-teaching performance.

The content of Time 3 is once again relevant to computer science. Transcript 6.9 below records what Manish says during this short segment of the micro-teaching.

TRANSCRIPT 6.9. Manish Channeling Steve Jobs

> so ↗↘OPERATING system *((writes and underlines words on board))* is
> something / that runs ↗↘PROGRAMS *((points to blank space on board))* /
> ↗↘PROGRAMS / correspond to some ↗↘JOBS *((moves left hand))* / sub-
> mitted by the ↗↘USERS *((moves both hands downward))* // so if you want
> to get something →DONE *((moves both hands downward and closes them))*
> / you create a ↗↘program / and you submit it to the ↗↘OPERATING
> system *((moves hands downward))* // the operating system ↗↘HANDLES
> *((moves right hand downward))* on how to ↗↘EXECUTE [Indian English
> stress pattern] it *((moves both hands downward))* / so ↗↘WHO *((opens
> hands widely))* executes that program *((smiles at audience))* // [1.4 sec-
> onds of pausing] in a computer that should be some ↗↘UNIT *((moves
> left hand outward))* / that is responsible for executing whatever you //
> [pause appears to be while thinking of the right word to say] whatever
> →JOB you submit right / so that should be some unit responsible for
> ↗↘HANDLING *((right hand moves downward))* that // [audience member
> says *uh huh*] that would be the ↗↘CPU *((points to CPU on board))*

In terms of non-verbal communication at Time 3, we see that Manish
is using several gestures to indicate prominent words: *jobs, users, done,
operating system, handles, execute,* and *unit.* Figure 6.17 shows Manish using
both hands to highlight the word *users.*

FIGURE 6.17. Manish Time 3 Gesturing for Prominent Word *users*

In addition, he invites interaction at Time 3, and he does so in two
ways: through a fairly long pause and by making eye contact and smiling
at the audience, much the same as he did when mirroring Steve Jobs (see
Figure 6.18 below).

FIGURE 6.18. Manish Time 3 Smile and Pause to Invite Interaction

Finally, just as Steve Jobs did with the visuals that he employed to introduce the new iPhone, Manish points to the board several times to draw the audience's attention to what is written there. Figure 6.19 illustrates his identification of the acronym *CPU*.

FIGURE 6.19. Manish Time 3 Indicating the Acronym *CPU* Written on Board

Manish's use of suprasegmentals, especially in terms of measures of fluency, are maintained at Time 3. His articulation rate is quite low at 4.5 syllables per second, and the mean length of runs in this segment of speech is 8.7 syllables. See Table 6.13 below for details.

TABLE 6.13. Manish Time 3 Measures of Fluency

	Time 3 Channeling
Total syllables	131 syllables
Total pause time	8.0 seconds (+ 0.6 seconds for audience response)
Total articulation time	37.9 seconds
Articulation rate (minus pause time)	4.5 syllables (131 syllables/37.9 – 8.6 seconds)
Mean length of run (syllables/ runs)	8.7 syllables/run (131 syllables/15 runs)

At Time 3, to deliver his own ideas, Manish has incorporated pausing, much as he did in his mirroring of Steve Jobs, and he has slowed down his speech rate to a rate that is much easier for U.S. audiences to follow. In addition, giving the audience time to process his questions and waiting for verbal responses has made his communication even more interactive and student-engaged.

Observable Changes From Time 1 to Time 3

This section summarizes Manish's improvement over the three time periods, focusing mainly on changes to his non-verbal communication and his pausing and rate of speech (measures of fluency).

Non-Verbal Communication

Table 6.14 below summarizes the changes in Manish's non-verbal communication from Time 1 (original micro-teaching) to Time 2 (mirroring) and Time 3 (channeling).

TABLE 6.14. Manish's Non-Verbal Communication at Times 1, 2, and 3

Time 1	Time 2	Time 3
Points to *algorithm analysis* on board.	Points towards imaginary screen.	Points to *CPU, operating system* on board.
One word is emphasized through gestures.	Employs more than 20 gestures to highlight prominent words and stressed syllables.	Employs gestures for nine prominent words and stressed syllables.
Smiles after posing a question to audience.	Smiles after giving introductory sentence.	Smiles after posing a rhetorical question.

Table 6.14 shows that Manish is using written support even during Time 1 although, if we look closely at Time 3, we observe that his white board becomes more clearly organized over time, including larger handwriting and a clearer connection between components. Through pointing to key words and concepts on the board, he does a better job of clearly showing the relationship between ideas. The biggest improvement, however, is his use of gestures to highlight prominent words and stressed syllables. At Time 1, we only find one word that is emphasized through use of gestures, whereas at Times 2 and 3, we see that Manish uses one or both hands in a downward movement to indicate several words that are prominent and syllables that are stressed, increasing substantially from Time 1 to Times 2 and 3. The major facial expression which he uses is a smile to indicate that he is connecting with his audience. Even though he smiles during each of the three recordings, his smiles at Time 3 with longer pauses (wait time) and use of shorter thought groups for questions make it more likely that audience members will respond to his initiation of interaction.

Suprasegmentals

Along with use of gesture to highlight prominent words and syllables, the biggest change for Manish in terms of suprasegmentals is in incorporating more pauses and in decreasing both his articulation rate and mean length of run. See Table 6.15 below for a comparison of Manish's temporal measures of fluency over the three time periods.

TABLE 6.15. Comparison of Measures of Fluency Times 1, 2, and 3 for Manish

	Time 1 (Diagnostic)	Time 2 (Mirroring)	Time 3 (Channeling)
Total syllables	73 syllables	97 syllables	131 syllables
Total pause time	2.1 seconds	19.8 seconds	8.0 secs (+ 0.6 seconds for audience response)
Total articulation time	16.0 seconds	45.5 seconds	37.9 seconds
Articulation rate (minus pause time)	**5.3 syllables** (73 syllables/16.0 secs – 2.1 seconds)	**3.8 syllables** (97 syllables/45.5 secs – 19.8 seconds)	**4.5 syllables** (131 syllables/37.9 secs – 8.6 seconds)
Mean length of run (syllables/runs)	**12.2 syllables** (73 syllables/6 runs)	**8.1 syllables** (97 syllables/12 runs)	**8.7 syllables** (131 syllables/15 runs)

There are two very noticeable improvements in this table. The first is that Manish's articulation rate has decreased from 5.3 syllables at Time 1 to a rate of 4.5 syllables at Time 3 (and this, while teaching and being rated!). On page 121, we mentioned that the ideal speaking rate for comprehensibility of speech is 4.7 for NSs and 4.2 for NNSs (Kang et al., 2010). At 4.5, Manish is clearly closer to the ideal. The second noticeable improvement is that the mean length of his runs has dropped from 12.2 syllables to 8.7 syllables, which is much closer to the recommended length of thought groups of between three and five words (Smith et al., 1992).

To sum up, we have seen that Manish is an ITA who presents quite different communication challenges compared to Kan-Ting. Whereas Kan-Ting needed to work on pitch variation, Manish needed to work on pausing and speech rate. Due to the individual nature of the MP, each ITA had the liberty to choose a model that benefitted himself the most in terms of his diagnosed weaknesses in delivery and communication.

Chapter 6 in Review

In this chapter, we have offered a detailed outline of the phases and steps to be taken in teaching with the MP, with the intention of making it possible for other instructors to use it with their own students. The three phases of *Analysis*, *Mirroring*, and *Channeling* are fleshed out in detail. We also provided guidance on how to find videos of speakers for students to use as models.

Following the introduction, the bulk of this chapter is devoted to two longitudinal case studies of ITAs we have taught, each of whom had different pronunciation needs related to intelligibility and delivery. Our intent was to show at a granular level how we used the MP to meet the learning needs of each individual in using this top-down pedagogical approach. "Kan-Ting" was a Mandarin and Taiwanese speaker working to improve his suprasegmentals and non-verbals, while "Manish" was bilingual in Tamil and Indian English, aiming to improve his intelligibility with U.S. American English interlocutors by working on his word stress and temporal measures of fluency. In each longitudinal case study, we documented the learners' progression through the sequential phases and steps of the MP, presenting evidence that their dramatic improvement in intelligibility and delivery was due to their internalization of the voices of their model speakers, as well as their subsequent ability to not just mimic the words of these speakers but to use the voices they internalized in the MP to communicate their own content in their disciplinary lectures. In doing so, the learners exhibited agency and initiative not just in selecting their model speakers, but in internalizing those speakers' stances to such an extent that their final performances embodied not just what those models had done, but what the learners imagined they might have done in delivering their disciplinary lectures (e.g., using gestures that were even more expansive than those seen in the model videos). In other words, the MP as a top-down approach empowered the learners to develop their own unique stance and voice as they improved their intelligibility and delivery.

Chapter 6 Notes

1. "Normal conversation moves between low and high pitch... The extra-high level ... is the pitch level often used in contrastive or emphatic stress" (Celce-Murcia et al., 2010, p. 230).
2. Interested readers are directed to view the approximately 16-minute TED Talk at https://www.ted.com/talks/anthony_atala_printing_a_human_kidney
3. While the entire keynote address is nearly two hours in length, Manish only selected a short segment to mirror. Interested readers will find the exact time signatures for this video marked in this chapter and are directed to the Apple Events Podcasts site to view this video at https://podcasts.apple.com/us/podcast/macworld-san-francisco-2007-keynote-address/id275834665?i=1000026524322

Chapter 7

Conclusion

In consideration of current L2 pronunciation teaching and learning goals (i.e., intelligibility as opposed to "nativeness"; Levis, 2018) and recent SLA theoretical frameworks emphasizing the role of social and contextual factors in shaping IL phonology, it is clear that a top-down approach is important in L2 pronunciation instruction. In this book, we have referenced the frequent observation that while children may succeed fairly easily, adults almost universally fail to achieve a native-like accent in their L2. The causes of this dramatic difference have been debated by bottom-up researchers, who attribute it to either the physical development of the brain or to identified stages of cognitive development, and by top-down variationist researchers, who suggest that accent signals ethnic and emotional identity, or ego, which is less "permeable" (Guiora et al., 1972) for adults than for children. Positioning ourselves with the top-down group, we have argued throughout this book that IL phonology is inextricably linked to a speaker's emotion and expression of identity, which we believe is usually less flexible for adults than for children.

Book Chapters in Review

Beginning with a review of bottom-up and top-down research on IL phonology and pronunciation in Chapter 2, we characterized the orientation taken in bottom-up SLA research on pronunciation as structuralist, focusing on the physical and linguistic forms of the stream of speech in isolation from the social context of speaking. In this orientation, the linguistic target in learning L2 phonology is assumed to be the standard accent of a NS of the L2, and L2 pronunciation learning is treated as a completely mental – perhaps even academic – process that is unaffected by social context. Issues were raised, however, about this mainstream research focus on native-like accent by a small body of U.S. researchers focused on the needs of ITAs, who observed that the pedagogical focus should not be whether these L2 learners had, or lacked a native-like accent but whether their speech was (or was not) intelligible to their audience of U.S. undergraduates. In researching what makes speech intelligible, these scholars identified not just specific phonemes, but prosodic features like intonation, stress, and rhythm in relation to the information structure of speech, in coordination with non-verbal features such as gesture, pausing, and use of space in interaction with interlocutors. Concurring with this line of research, we explored this kind of top-down approach to teaching pronunciation as an alternative to the bottom-up approach often used in the research and teaching of L2s. As we suggested in Chapter 2, the fact that the growing population of L2 learners with emergent literacy is less able to benefit from bottom-up instruction provides an added incentive to our exploration of alternative top-down orientations for teaching pronunciation.

Replacing native accent as the goal of instruction with the two related goals of intelligibility and a TL accent that expresses a learner's identity, we provided a detailed account in Chapter 3 of research on intelligibility and accentedness of L2 learners in the workplace. Addressing these two goals, we first reviewed three major factors that improve intelligibility and comprise a speaker's delivery (Yates, 2017): pronunciation, non-verbal communication, and pragmatics. Then, we reviewed replacement of native accent as the target of instruction with a TL accent that expresses a learner's identity; we provided a detailed review of research showing that IL phonology is uniquely tied to the surrounding social context and to expressions of speaker identity and desired group membership.

In Chapter 4, we examined the process of phonological "style-shifting" when speakers choose whether or not to accommodate to and/or parody the phonological patterns of others for purposes of impression management or language play. According to SCT, the language we are exposed to in our social environments is internalized along with elements of its original social context, constituting what Bakhtin (1934/1981) and others have referred to as *voices*. Over time, these voices become accessible to the speaker as cognitive resources/tools which can be invoked at will for new purposes. In this way, speakers exert agency in performing the identities of others by means of vocal stylization (or double voicing) to manage others' impressions of them (Goffman, 1959; Yates, 2017). The findings of the studies reviewed in Chapter 4 raise important pedagogical implications for L2 pronunciation instruction; most importantly, how can teachers create a space for their students to adopt and internalize a range of such voices (including more target-like voices) as resources available to use for their own purposes? The theoretical frameworks and research findings reviewed in the first half of this book point to the benefits of using a top-down, holistic teaching approach to the teaching of L2 pronunciation – one that accepts the idea of a multi-voiced IL competence – to enable a learner to shift pronunciation to enact different L2 voices that signal each speaker's emotion, personal stance, and identification with different speech communities.

Building on the work of such scholars on pedagogy such as the Douglas Fir Group (2016), Moyer (2017), Müller (2013), Pennington and Richards (1986), and Yates (2017), Chapter 5 presented a synthesized list of teaching recommendations for top-down pronunciation instruction, conveniently indexed in Table 5.1 shown on page 69. We described and critiqued the different top-down approaches and activities to teaching pronunciation that have been described in the literature, including those engaging such methods as tracking and shadowing as well as role-play and other drama techniques.

Finally, in Chapter 6, we provided a detailed account of the Mirroring Project – an effective top-down pedagogical approach for L2 pronunciation instruction. We described two case studies in detail to demonstrate how this project helps learners internalize and then use the voices (including non-verbals and emotional stances) of self-selected role models for their own purposes. We showed how students in the MP worked towards meeting their own unique goals in pronunciation, pragmatics, and identity expression as they selected and re-enacted the voices of video-recorded speakers they had chosen, focusing on their identity expression, emotion, and pragmatic goals. Following their analysis and attempt to move and speak like their selected models, students learned to "channel" that voice – the discursive, non-verbal and pragmatic features of their model – to deliver their own messages. They then reflected on what it felt like to speak to their target audience with that voice, to improve their intelligibility, delivery, and expression of identity in their target speech community.

Closing Remarks

In this book, we have presented a research-based case for prioritizing intelligibility and stance as important goals in the learning and teaching of L2 pronunciation. We hope to have persuaded teachers of L2 pronunciation to add top-down approaches as an essential part of their pedagogy (and particularly when their students have emergent levels of alphabetic print literacy). In particular, we hope that teachers reading this book will undertake MPs with their own group of students. The authors have used this project in their classes over the course of more than 20 years, and have presented before and after videos on it numerous times at international conferences to very appreciative audiences. The overwhelming response of students has been highly favorable; comments range from the MP being the highlight of the semester to suggestions that future students do several MPs because the activity has been so beneficial. It is always entertaining to meet someone from a previous semester who, even years later, quotes verbatim from their project, still using the same prosodic patterns and non-verbals that they learned in the class. We believe that such encounters vividly demonstrate how the MP can empower learners to exert agency in developing their own unique stance and voice as they improve their intelligibility by internalizing the voices of others who have left a lasting impression on them. In that regard, we encourage practicing teachers – in whatever L2 teaching context(s) they find themselves – to try out this activity in their own classrooms. We truly hope that they and their students will enjoy and benefit from this pedagogical approach as much as we have. Such top-down approaches to pronunciation pedagogy, strongly supported by the research we have cited, should be a central component of all L2 pronunciation pedagogy.

References

Abercrombie, D. (1968). Paralanguage. *British Journal of Disorders of Communication,* *3*(1), 55–59. https://doi.org/10.3109/13682826809011441

Acton, W. (1984). Changing fossilized pronunciation. *TESOL Quarterly, 18*(1), 71–85. https://doi.org/10.2307/3586336

Anderson-Hsieh, J. (1990). Teaching suprasegmentals to international teaching assistants using field-specific materials. *English for Specific Purposes, 9*(3), 195–214. https://doi.org/10.1016/0889-4906(90)90013-3

Atala, A. (2011). *Printing a human kidney* [Video]. TED. Accessed 21 August 2021 at https://www.ted.com/talks/anthony_atala_printing_a_human_kidney

Avery, P., & Ehrlich, S. (1992). *Teaching American English pronunciation.* Oxford University Press.

Bakhtin, M. (1981). *The dialogic imagination: Four essays by M. M. Bakhtin.* M. Holquist (Ed.). (C. Emerson & M. Holquist, Trans.). University of Texas Press. (Original work published in Russian in 1934.)

Bakhtin, M. (1984). *Problems of Dostoevsky's poetics.* C. Emerson (Ed. and Trans.). Manchester University Press. (Original work published in Russian in 1963.)

Bardovi-Harlig, K. (2013). Developing L2 pragmatics. *Language Learning, 63*(S1), 68–86. https://doi.org/10.1111/j.1467-9922.2012.00738.x

Beebe, L. (1977). The influence of the listener on code-switching. *Language Learning, 27*(2), 331–339. https://doi.org/10.1111/j.1467-1770.1977.tb00125.x

Beebe, L. (1980). Sociolinguistic variation and style shifting in second language acquisition. *Language Learning, 30*(2), 433–445. https://doi.org/10.1111/j.1467-1770.1980.tb00327.x

Beebe, L. (1981). Social and situational factors influencing the communicative strategy of dialect code-switching. *International Journal of the Sociology of Language, 32,* 139–149. https://doi.org/10.1515/ijsl.1981.32.139

Beebe, L. (1982). *The social psychological basis of style shifting* [Plenary address]. Second Language Research Forum, Los Angeles, CA.

Beebe, L., & Giles, H. (1984). Speech-accommodation theories: A discussion in terms of second-language acquisition. *International Journal of the Sociology of Language, 46,* 5–32. https://doi.org/10.1515/ijsl.1984.46.5

Bell, A. (1984). Language style as audience design. *Language in Society, 13*(2), 145–204. https://doi.org/10.1017/S004740450001037X

Belz, J. (2002). Second language play as a representation of the multicompetent self in foreign language study. *Journal of Language, Identity & Education, 1*(1), 13–39. https://doi.org/10.1207/S15327701JLIE0101_3

Blackledge, A., & Creese, A. (2014). Heteroglossia as practice and pedagogy. In A. Blackledge & A. Creese (Eds.), *Heteroglossia as practice and pedagogy* (pp. 1–20). Springer.

Block, D. (2003). *The social turn in second language acquisition.* Georgetown University Press.

Boersma, P., & Weenink, D. (n.d.). *Praat: Doing phonetics by computer.* Accessed 21 August 2021 at http://www.praat.org/

Bondevik, S.-G. (1996). *Foreigner talk revisited: When does it really occur and why?* [Unpublished M.A. thesis]. University of Tromsø, Norway.

Brazil, D. (1997). *The communicative value of intonation in English.* Cambridge University Press. (Original work published in 1985 by the English Language Research Unit, University of Birmingham.)

Brière, E. (1966). An investigation of phonological interference. *Language, 42*(4), 768–796. https://doi.org/10.2307/411832

Broner, M., & Tarone, E. (2001). Is it fun? Language play in a fifth-grade Spanish immersion classroom. *The Modern Language Journal, 85*(3), 363–379. https://doi.org/10.1111/0026-7902.00114

Brown, G. (1977). *Listening to spoken English.* Longman.

Brown, G., & Yule, G. (1983). *Discourse analysis.* Cambridge University Press.

Byrd, P., Constantinides, J., & Pennington, M. C. (1989). *The foreign teaching assistant's manual.* Collier Macmillan.

Canale, M., & Swain, M. (1980). Theoretical bases of communicative approaches to second language teaching and testing. *Applied Linguistics, 1*(1), 1–47. https://doi.org/10.1093/applin/I.1.1

Carkin, G. (2004). Drama for pronunciation. *Compleat Links, 1*(5). Accessed 21 August 2021 at https://www.tesol.org/read-and-publish/journals/other-serial-publications/compleat-links/compleat-links-volume-1-issue-5-(winter-2004)/drama-for-pronunciation

Carkin, G. (2005a). *Ten MORE Plays for the ESL/EFL Classroom.* Carlisle Publications.

Carkin, G. (2005b). *Using plays for pronunciation practice: Acting and English in seven easy steps* [Plenary address]. TESOL-France Colloquium. Paris.

Carkin, G. (2007). *Teaching English through drama: The state of the art.* Carlisle Publications.

Carkin, G., Hall, D., & Day, C. (2003). *Ten plays for the ESL/EFL classroom.* Carlisle Publications.

Catford, J. C. (1964). Phonation types: The classification of some laryngeal components of speech production. In D. Abercrombie, D. B. Fry, P. A. D. MacCarthy, N. C. Scott, & J. L. M. Trim (Eds.), *In honour of Daniel Jones: Papers contributed on the occasion of his eightieth birthday 12 September 1961* (pp. 26–37). Longmans.

Celce-Murcia, M., Brinton, D. M., & Goodwin, J. M. (2010). *Teaching pronunciation: A course book and reference guide* (2nd ed.). Cambridge University Press.

Chomsky, N. (1957). *Syntactic structures*. Mouton.

Chomsky, N. (1959). Review of B. F. Skinner, Verbal behavior. *Language, 35*(1), 26–58. https://doi.org/10.2307/411334

Chomsky, N. (1988). *Language and the problem of knowledge: The Managua lectures*. MIT Press.

Clark, H. H., & Gerrig, R. J. (1990). Quotations as demonstrations. *Language, 66*(4), 764–805. https://doi.org/10.2307/414729

Cohen, A., Collier, R., & 't Hart, J. (1982). Declination: Construct or intrinsic feature of speech pitch? *Phonetica, 39*(4–5), 254–273. https://doi.org/10.1159/000261666

Coleman, L. (2005). *Drama-based English as a foreign language instruction for Korean adolescents* [Unpublished doctoral dissertation]. Pepperdine University, United States.

Dahm, M. R., & Yates, L. (2013). English for the workplace: Doing patient-centred care in medical communication. *TESL Canada Journal, 30*(7), 21–44. https://doi.org/10.18806/tesl.v30i7.1150

Dalton, C., & Seidlhofer, B. (2000). *Language teaching: A scheme for teacher education* (3rd ed.). Oxford University Press.

Dauer, R. M. (1983). Stress-timing and syllable-timing reanalyzed. *Journal of Phonetics, 11*(1), 51–62. https://doi.org/10.1016/S0095-4470(19)30776-4

Derwing, T. M. (2016). The three P's of ESL in the workplace: Proficiency, pronunciation & pragmatics. *CONTACT, 42*(2), 10–20. Accessed 21 August 2021 at http://contact.teslontario.org/issues/research-symposium-2016/

Derwing, T. M., & Munro, M. J. (2009). Comprehensibility as a factor in listener interaction preferences: Implications for the workplace. *The Canadian Modern Language Review, 66*(2), 181–202. https://doi.org/10.3138/cmlr.66.2.181

Derwing, T. M., & Munro, M. J. (2015). *Pronunciation fundamentals: Evidence-based perspectives for L2 teaching and research*. John Benjamins.

Derwing, T. M., Munro, M. J., Foote, J. A., Waugh, E., & Fleming, J. (2014). Opening the window on comprehensible pronunciation after 19 years: A workplace training study. *Language Learning, 64*(3), 526–548. https://doi.org/10.1111/lang.12053

Derwing, T. M., Munro, M. J., & Thomson, R. I. (2008). A longitudinal study of ESL learners' fluency and comprehensibility development. *Applied Linguistics, 29*(3), 359–380. https://doi.org/10.1093/applin/amm041

Derwing, T. M., Waugh, E., & Munro, M. J. (2021). Pragmatically speaking: Preparing adult ESL students for the workplace. *Applied Pragmatics, 3*(2), 107–135. https://doi.org/10.1075/ap.20001.der

Dickerson, L. (1975). The learner's interlanguage as a system of variable rules. *TESOL Quarterly, 9*(4), 401–407. https://doi.org/10.2307/3585624

Dickerson, L., & Dickerson, W. (1977). Interlanguage phonology: Current research and future directions. In S. P. Corder & E. Roulet (Eds.), *Interlanguages and pidgins and their relationship to second language pedagogy* (pp. 18–30). Libraire Droz Neufchatel.

Dickerson, W. (1989). Stress in the speech stream: The rhythm of spoken English. The University of Illinois Press.

Dittman, A. T. (1974). The body movement-speech rhythm relationship as a cue to speech encoding. In S. Weitz (Ed.), *Nonverbal communication* (pp. 169–181). Oxford University Press.

Douglas Fir Group. (2016). A transdisciplinary framework for SLA in a multilingual world. *The Modern Language Journal, 100*(S1), 19–47. https://doi.org/10.1111/modl.12301

Eckert, P., & Rickford, J. R. (Eds.). (2001). *Style and sociolinguistic variation*. Cambridge University Press.

Eckman, F. (1977). Markedness and the contrastive analysis hypothesis. *Language Learning, 27*(2), 315–330. https://doi.org/10.1111/j.1467-1770.1977.tb00124.x

Eckman, F. (1991). The structural conformity hypothesis and the acquisition of consonant clusters in the interlanguage of ESL learners. *Studies in Second Language Acquisition, 13*(1), 23–41. https://doi.org/10.1017/S0272263100009700

Ellis, R. (1985). A variable competence model of second language acquisition. *International Review of Applied Linguistics in Language Teaching, 23*(1–4), 47–70. https://doi.org/10.1515/iral.1985.23.1-4.47

Ellis, R. (1990). A response to Gregg. *Applied Linguistics, 11*(4), 384–391. https://doi.org/10.1093/applin/11.4.384

Ellis, R. (2008). *The study of second language acquisition* (2nd ed.). Oxford University Press.

Fasold, R., & Preston, D. R. (2007). The psycholinguistic unity of inherent variability: Old Occam whips out his razor. In R. Bayley & C. Lucas (Eds.), *Sociolinguistic variation: Theory, methods and applications* (pp. 45–69). Cambridge University Press.

Ferré, G. (2018). Gesture/speech integration in the perception of prosodic emphasis. In K. Klessa, J. Bachan, A. Wagner, M. Karpiński, & D. Śledziński (Eds.), *Proceedings of the 9th International Conference on Speech Prosody* (pp. 35–39). International Speech Communication Association.

Ferré, G. (2019). Time reference in weather reports: The contribution of gesture in French and English. In I. Galhano-Rodrigues, E. Z. Galvão, & A. Cruz-Santos (Eds.), *Recent perspectives on gesture and multimodality* (pp. 31–40). Cambridge Scholars.

Finger, A. (1999). *The magic of drama: An oral performance activity book*. Full Blast Productions.

Firth, A., & Wagner, J. (1997). On discourse, communication, and (some) fundamental concepts in SLA research. *The Modern Language Journal, 81*(3), 285–300. https://doi.org/10.2307/329302

Flege, J. E. (1987). The production of "new" and "similar" phones in a foreign language: Evidence for the effect of equivalence classification. *Journal of Phonetics, 15*(1), 47–65. https://doi.org/10.1016/S0095-4470(19)30537-6

Flege, J. E., Bohn, O.-S., & Jang, S. (1997). Effects of experience on non-native speakers' production and perception of English vowels. *Journal of Phonetics, 25*(4), 437–470. https://doi.org/10.1006/jpho.1997.0052

Flip. (2022). Accessed 30 August, 2022 at https://info.flip.com/

Foote, J. A. (2015). *Pronunciation and speech perception: Three studies.* [Unpublished doctoral dissertation]. Concordia University, Canada. Accessed 21 August 2021 at https://spectrum.library.concordia.ca/980242/

Foote, J. A., & McDonough, K. (2017). Using shadowing with mobile technology to improve L2 pronunciation. *Journal of Second Language Pronunciation, 3*(1), 34–56. https://doi.org/10.1075/jslp.3.1.02foo

Forman, M. (Director). Zaents, S., Douglas, M. (Producers). (1975). *One flew over the cuckoo's nest* [Motion picture]. Fantasy Films.

Forman, R. (2011). Humorous language play in a Thai EFL classroom. *Applied Linguistics, 32*(5), 541–565. https://doi.org/10.1093/applin/amr022

Galante, A., & Thomson, R. (2017). The effectiveness of drama as an instructional approach for the development of second language oral fluency, comprehensibility, and accentedness. *TESOL Quarterly, 51*(1), 115–142. https://doi.org/10.1002/tesq.290

Garber, M. (2015, Feb. 6). Foucault that noise: The terror of highbrow mispronunciation. *The Atlantic.* Accessed 21 August 2021 at https://www.theatlantic.com/entertainment/archive/2015/02/foucault-that-noise-the-terror-of-highbrow-mispronunciation/385229/

Gatbonton, E., Trofimovich, P., & Magid, M. (2005). Learners' ethnic group affiliation and L2 pronunciation accuracy: A sociolinguistic investigation. *TESOL Quarterly, 39*(3), 489–511. https://doi.org/10.2307/3588491

Gilbert, J. (1987). Pronunciation and listening comprehension. In J. Morley (Ed.), *Current perspectives on pronunciation* (pp. 33–39). Teachers of English to Speakers of Other Languages.

Giles, H. (2016). *Communication accommodation theory: Negotiating personal relationships and social identities across contexts.* Cambridge University Press.

Goffman, E. (1959). *The presentation of self in everyday life.* Anchor Doubleday.

Gorsuch, G., Meyers, C., Pickering, L., & Griffee, D. T. (2013). *English communication for international teaching assistants* (2nd ed.). Waveland Press.

Gregg, K. (1990). The variable competence model of second language acquisition and why it isn't. *Applied Linguistics, 11*(4), 364–383. https://doi.org/10.1093/applin/11.4.364

Gregg, K. (1993). Taking explanation seriously; or, let a couple of flowers bloom. *Applied Linguistics, 14*(3), 276–294. https://doi.org/10.1093/applin/14.3.276

Guiora, A., Beit-Hallahmi, R., Brannon, R., Dull, C., & Scovel, T. (1972). The effects of experimentally induced changes in ego states on pronunciation ability in a second language: An exploratory study. *Comprehensive Psychiatry, 13*(5), 421–428. https://doi.org/10.1016/0010-440x(72)90083-1

Gumperz, J. (1982). *Discourse strategies.* Cambridge University Press.

Hahn, L. D. (2004). Primary stress and intelligibility: Research to motivate the teaching of suprasegmentals. *TESOL Quarterly, 38*(2), 201–223. https://doi.org/10.2307/3588378

Halliday, M. A. K. (1985). *Spoken and written language.* Oxford University Press.

Hardison, D. M. (2016). *Visualizing the gesture and the prosodic components of emphasis in oral discourse* [Plenary address]. 8th Annual Conference of Pronunciation in Second Language Learning and Teaching (PSLLT), University of Calgary, Canada.

Hastings, A., & Manning, P. (2004). Introduction: Acts of alterity. *Language & Communication, 24*(4), 291–311. https://doi.org/10.1016/j.langcom.2004.07.001

Henrichsen, L. (2015). Video voiceovers for helpful, enjoyable pronunciation practice. In J. Levis, R. Mohammed, M. Qian, & Z. Zhou (Eds.), *Proceedings of the 6th Pronunciation in Second Language Learning and Teaching Conference* (pp. 270–276). Iowa State University.

Hewings, M. (1995). Tone choice in the English intonation of non-native speakers. *International Review of Applied Linguistics, 33*(3), 251–284. https://doi.org/10.1515/iral.1995.33.3.251

Hinofotis, F., & Bailey, K. (1978). Course development: Oral communication for advanced university ESL students. In J. Povey (Ed.), *UCLA Workpapers in Teaching English as a Second Language, 12* (pp. 7–20). University of California.

Hinofotis, F., & Bailey, K. (1981). American undergraduates' reactions to the communication skills of foreign teaching assistants. In J. Fisher, M. Clarke, & J. Schacter (Eds.), *On TESOL '80: Building bridges: Research and practice in teaching English as a second language* (pp. 120–136). Teachers of English to Speakers of Other Languages.

Hoffman, E. (1989). *Lost in translation: A life in a new language.* E. P. Dutton.

House, A. S. (1961). On vowel duration in English. *Journal of the Acoustical Society of America, 33,* 1174–1178. https://doi.org/10.1121/1.1908941

Huang, H.-Y. C., & Tseng, C.-J. (2021). The effects of film-dubbing technique on the comprehensibility of Taiwanese EFL learners. *TESOL Journal, 12,* e565. https://doi.org/10.1002/tesj.565

Hymes, D. (1972). On communicative competence. In J. B. Price & J. Holmes (Eds.), *Sociolinguistics* (pp. 269–293). Penguin Books.

Isaacs, T., & Trofimovich, P. (2012). Deconstructing comprehensibility: Identifying the linguistic influences on listeners' L2 comprehensibility ratings. *Studies in Second Language Acquisition, 34*(3), 475–505. https://doi.org/10.1017/S0272263112000150

Jenkins, J. (2000). *The phonology of English as an international language.* Oxford University Press.

Jobs, S. (2007). Macworld San Francisco 2007 keynote address [Video]. Apple Events. Accessed 2 February 2022 at https://podcasts.apple.com/us/podcast/macworld-san-francisco-2007-keynote-address/id275834665?i=1000026524322

Johansson, F. A. (1973). *Immigrant Swedish phonology: A study in multiple contact analysis.* CWK Gleerup.

Kang, O., Rubin, D., & Pickering, L. (2010). Suprasegmental measures of accentedness and judgments of language learner proficiency in oral English. *The Modern Language Journal, 94*(4), 554–566. https://doi.org/10.1111/j.1540–4781.2010.01091.x

Kao, S. (1994). *Classroom interaction in a drama-oriented English conversation class of first-year college students in Taiwan: A teacher-researcher study* [Unpublished doctoral dissertation]. The Ohio State University, United States.

Key, M. R. (1980). *The relationship of verbal and non-verbal communication.* De Gruyter Mouton.

Kiesling, S. F. (2005). Variation, stance and style: Word-final *-er*, high rising tone, and ethnicity in Australian English. *English World-Wide, 26*(1), 1–42. https://doi.org/10.1075/eww.26.1.02kie

Kiesling, S. F. (2009). Style as stance: Stance as the explanation for patterns of sociolinguistic variation. In A. Jaffe (Ed.), *Stance: Sociolinguistic perspectives* (pp. 171–194). Oxford University Press.

Kiesling, S. F. (2019). The "gay voice" and "brospeak": Toward a systematic model of stance. In K. Hall & R. Barrett (Eds.), *The Oxford handbook of language and sexuality.* Oxford University Press [online version]. https://doi.org/10.1093/oxfordhb/9780190212926.013.11

Kormos, J. (1999). Monitoring and self-repair in L2. *Language Learning, 49*(2), 303–342. https://doi.org/10.1111/0023-8333.00090

Krashen, S. (1973). Lateralization, language learning, and the critical period: Some new evidence. *Language Learning, 23*(1), 63–74. https://doi.org/10.1111/j.1467-1770.1973.tb00097.x

Krashen, S. (1981). *Second language acquisition and second language learning.* Pergamon Press.

Krashen, S. (1982). *Principles and practice in second language acquisition.* Pergamon Press.

Kreidler, C. (1989). *The pronunciation of English: A course book in phonology.* Blackwell.

Labov, W. (1970). The study of language in its social context. *Studium Generale, 23,* 30–87.

Labov, W. (1972). *Sociolinguistic patterns.* University of Pennsylvania Press.

Ladd, D. R. (1984). Declination: A review and some hypotheses. *Phonology, 1,* 53–74. https://doi.org/10.1017/S0952675700000294

Lado, R., & Fries, C. (1958). *English pronunciation: Exercises in sound segments, intonation, and rhythm.* University of Michigan Press.

Lantolf, J. P. (Ed.). (2000). *Sociocultural theory and second language learning.* Oxford University Press.

Lantolf, J. P. (2006). Sociocultural theory and L2: State of the art. *Studies in Second Language Acquisition, 28*(1), 67–109. https://doi.org/10.1017/S0272263106060037

Lantolf, J. P., & Beckett, T. (2009). Sociocultural theory and second language acquisition. *Language Teaching, 42*(4), 459–475. https://doi.org/10.1017/S0261444809990048

Lantolf, J. P., & Thorne, S. L. (2006). *Sociocultural theory and the genesis of second language development.* Oxford University Press.

Lantolf, J. P., Thorne, S. L., & Poehner, M. (2015). Sociocultural theory and second language development. In B. VanPatten & J. Williams (Eds.), *Theories in second language acquisition: An introduction* (2nd ed., pp. 207–226). Routledge/Taylor & Francis.

Larsen-Freeman, D. (1975). The acquisition of grammatical morphemes by adult ESL students. *TESOL Quarterly, 9*(4), 409–419. https://doi.org/10.2307/3585625

LaScotte, D. (2016). *'So please be nice in class!': An analysis of the complexity, accuracy and fluency of two English learners' language through a heteroglossic lens* [Unpublished M.A. qualifying paper]. University of Minnesota, United States. Accessed 21 August 2021 at University of Minnesota Digital Conservancy, http://hdl.handle.net/11299/179951

LaScotte, D. (2019). Enacting voices: An analysis on the complexity, accuracy, and fluency of heteroglossic speech. *Journal of Second Language Studies, 2*(1), 45–70. https://doi.org/10.1075/jsls.17027.las

LaScotte, D. (2022). L2 voices and materials as tools in pronunciation pedagogy. In D. LaScotte, C. Mathieu, & S. David (Eds.), *New perspectives on material mediation in language learner pedagogy* (pp. 267–286). Springer.

LaScotte, D., Meyers, C., & Tarone, E. (2021). Voice and mirroring in SLA: Top-down pedagogy for L2 pronunciation instruction. *RELC Journal, 52*(1), 144–154. https://doi.org/10.1177/0033688220953910

LaScotte, D., & Tarone, E. (2019). Heteroglossia and constructed dialogue in SLA. *The Modern Language Journal, 103*(S1), 95–112. https://doi.org/10.1111/modl.12533

LaScotte, D., & Tarone, E. (in press). Channeling "voices" to improve L2 English intelligibility. *The Modern Language Journal, 106*(4).

Laver, J. (1980). *The phonemic description of voice quality.* Cambridge University Press.

Lenneberg, E. (1967). *Biological foundations of language.* John Wiley and Sons.

LESLLA. (n.d.). Literacy Education and Second Language Learning for Adults (LESLLA). https://www.leslla.org/our-vision

Lessac, A. (1967). *The use and training of the human voice* (2nd ed.). Drama Book Specialists.

LeVelle, K., & Levis, J. (2014). Understanding the impact of social factors on L2 pronunciation: Insights from learners. In J. Levis & A. Moyer (Eds.), *Social factors in L2 pronunciation* (pp. 97–118). De Gruyter Mouton.

Levis, J. M. (2005). Changing contexts and shifting paradigms in pronunciation teaching. *TESOL Quarterly, 39*(3), 369–377. https://doi.org/10.2307/3588485

Levis, J. M. (2018). *Intelligibility, oral communication, and the teaching of pronunciation.* Cambridge University Press.

Lindgren, J., Meyers, C., & Monk, M. (2003). *Approaches to accent: The Mirroring Project* [Conference presentation]. TESOL 2003 International Convention & English Language Expo, Baltimore, MD.

Liu, G.-Q. (1991). *Interaction and second language acquisition: A case study of a Chinese child's acquisition of English as a second language* [Unpublished doctoral dissertation]. La Trobe University, Australia.

LoCoco, V. (1976). A comparison of three methods for the collection of L2 data: Free composition, translation, and picture description. *Working Papers in Bilingualism, 8*, 59–86. Ontario Institute for Studies in Education.

Long, M. (1990). Maturational constraints on language development. *Studies in Second Language Acquisition, 12*(3), 251–285. https://doi.org/10.1017/S0272263100009165

Long, M. (1998). SLA: Breaking the siege. *University of Hawai'i Working Papers in ESL, 17*, 79–129. University of Hawai'i.

Lybeck, K. (2002). Cultural identification and second language pronunciation of Americans in Norway. *The Modern Language Journal, 86*(2), 174–191. https://doi.org/10.1111/1540-4781.00143

Major, R. C. (2001). *Foreign accent: The ontogeny and phylogeny of second language phonology*. Lawrence Erlbaum.

Marsh, J. (1981). Social factors of language use in physician–patient interaction. In D. Sankoff & H. Cedergren (Eds.), *Variation omnibus* (pp. 545–562). Linguistics Research, Inc.

Martinsen, R., Montgomery, C., & Willardson, V. (2017). The effectiveness of video-based shadowing and tracking pronunciation exercises for foreign language learners. *Foreign Language Annals, 50*(4), 661–680. https://doi.org/10.1111/flan.12306

Marx, N. (2002). Never quite a 'native speaker': Accent and identity in the L2 – and the L1. *The Canadian Modern Language Review, 59*(2), 264–281. https://doi.org/10.3138/cmlr.59.2.264

Mathis, T., & Yule, G. (1994). Zero quotatives. *Discourse Processes, 18*(1), 63–76. https://doi.org/10.1080/01638539409544884

McNeill, D. (1985). So you think gestures are nonverbal? *Psychological Review, 92*(3), 350–371. https://doi.apa.org/doi/10.1037/0033-295X.92.3.350

McNeill, D. (1992). *Hand and mind*. University of Chicago Press.

Mestenhauser, J., Perry, W., Paige, M., Landa, M., Brutsch, S., Dege, D., Doyle, K., Gillette, S., Hughes, G., Judy, R., Keye, Z., Murphy, K., Smith, J., Vandersluis, K., & Wendt, J. (1980). *Report of a special course for foreign student teaching assistants to improve their classroom effectiveness*. University of Minnesota International Student Adviser's Office and Program in English as a Second Language.

Meyers, C. (2013). Mirroring project update: Intelligible accented speakers as pronunciation models. *TESOL Video News*. Accessed 21 August 2021 at http://newsmanager.commpartners.com/tesolvdmis/issues/2013-07-27/6.html

Meyers, C. (2014). Intelligible accented speakers as pronunciation models. In J. Levis & S. McCrocklin (Eds.), *Proceedings of the 5th Pronunciation in Second Language Learning and Teaching Conference* (pp. 172–76). Iowa State University.

Meyers, C. (2018). Mirroring a TED talk. In E. Tarone (Chair), *Voices in learner language: Heteroglossia, language play and constructed dialogue in SLA* [Panel presentation]. Annual Conference of the American Association for Applied Linguistics, Chicago, IL.

Milroy, L. (1987). *Language and social networks* (2nd ed.). Blackwell.

Mitschke, C., & Tano, C. (2011). *D'accord!* Vista Higher Learning.

Monk, M. (2002). *The imitation project* [Conference presentation]. TESOL 2002 International Convention & English Language Expo, Salt Lake City, UT.

Monk, M., Lindgren, J., & Meyers, C. (2004). *Documenting prosodic acquisition with the mirroring technique* [Conference presentation]. TESOL 2004 International Convention & English Language Expo, Long Beach, CA.

Moreno, L. (2016). *Channeling Charlie: Suprasegmental pronunciation in a second language learner's performance of others' voices* [Unpublished M.A. qualifying paper]. University of Minnesota, United States. Accessed 21 August 2021 at University of Minnesota Digital Conservancy, http://hdl.handle.net/11299/183052

Morgan, B. (1997). Identity and intonation: Linking dynamic processes in an ESL classroom. *TESOL Quarterly, 31*(3), 431–450. https://doi.org/10.2307/3587833

Morley, J. (1991). The pronunciation component of teaching English to speakers of other languages. *TESOL Quarterly, 25*(3), 481–520. https://doi.org/10.2307/3586981

Moyer, A. (2017). Autonomy in second language phonology: Choice vs. limits. *Language Teaching, 50*(3), 395–411. https://doi.org/10.1017/S0261444815000191

Muir, C., Dörnyei, Z., & Adolphs, S. (2021). Role models in language learning: Results of a large-scale international survey. *Applied Linguistics, 42*(1), 1–23. https://doi.org/10.1093/applin/amz056

Müller, M. (2013). Conceptualizing pronunciation as part of translingual/transcultural competence: New impulses for SLA research and the L2 classroom. *Foreign Language Annals, 46*(2), 213–229. https://doi.org/10.1111/flan.12024

Munro, M. J., & Derwing, T. M. (1995). Foreign accent, comprehensibility, and intelligibility in the speech of second language learners. *Language Learning, 45*(1), 73–97. https://doi.org/10.1111/j.1467-1770.1995.tb00963.x

Munro, M. J., & Derwing, T. M. (2001). Modeling perceptions of the accentedness and comprehensibility of L2 speech: The role of speaking rate. *Studies in Second Language Acquisition, 23*(4), 451–468. https://doi.org/10.1017/S0272263101004016

Munro, M. J., Derwing, T. M., & Morton, S. L. (2006). The mutual intelligibility of L2 speech. *Studies in Second Language Acquisition, 28*(1), 111–131. https://doi.org/10.1017/S0272263106060049

Murphy, J. (2012). Models of pronunciation teaching: Accented, intelligible, comprehensible ESL speakers [Conference presentation]. TESOL 2012 International Convention & English Language Expo, Philadelphia, PA.

Murphy, J. (2014). Intelligible, comprehensible, non-native models in ESL/EFL pronunciation teaching. *System, 42*, 258–269. https://doi.org/10.1016/j.system.2013.12.007

Nadasdi, T. (1995). Subject NP doubling, matching, and minority French. *Language Variation and Change, 7*(1), 1–14. https://doi.org/10.1017/S0954394500000879

Nemser, W. (1971). *An experimental study of phonological interference in the English of Hungarians.* Indiana University Press.

New International Version Bible. (1978). Biblica. Accessed 21 August 2021 at https://www.biblica.com/bible/niv/judges/12/

Oller, D. K. (1974a). *Toward a general theory of phonological processes in first and second language learning* [Plenary address]. Western Conference on Linguistics, Seattle, WA.

Oller, D. K. (1974b). Simplification as the goal of phonological processes in child speech. *Language Learning, 24*(2), 299–303. https://doi.org/10.1111/j.1467-1770.1974.tb00510.x

Pavlenko, A., & Norton, B. (2007). Imagined communities, identity, and English language learning. In J. Cummins & C. Davison (Eds.), *International handbook of English language teaching* (pp. 669–680). Springer.

Pennington, M. C. (1989). Teaching pronunciation from the top down. *RELC Journal, 20*(1), 20–38. https://doi.org/10.1177/003368828902000103

Pennington, M. C., & Ellis, N. C. (2000). Cantonese speakers' memory for English sentences with prosodic cues. *The Modern Language Journal, 84*(3), 372–389. https://doi.org/10.1111/0026-7902.00075

Pennington, M. C., & Richards, J. C. (1986). Pronunciation revisited. *TESOL Quarterly, 20*(2), 207–225. https://doi.org/10.2307/3586541

Pennycook, A. (1985). Actions speak louder than words: Paralanguage, communication, and education. *TESOL Quarterly, 19*(2), 259–282. https://doi.org/10.2307/3586829

Pica, T., Gregory, A. B., & Finger, A. G. (1990). *Teaching matters: Skills and strategies for International Teaching Assistants.* Newbury House.

Pickering, L. (2001). The role of tone choice in improving ITA communication in the classroom. *TESOL Quarterly, 35*(2), 233–255. https://doi.org/10.2307/3587647

Pickering, L. (2012). Intonation. In K. Malmkjaer (Ed.), *The Routledge Linguistics Encyclopedia* (3rd ed., pp. 280–286). Routledge.

Pickering, L. (2018). *Discourse intonation: A discourse-pragmatic approach to teaching the pronunciation of English.* University of Michigan Press.

Pienemann, M. (1998). *Language processing and second language development.* John Benjamins.

Pike, K. L. (1945). *The intonation of American English.* University of Michigan Press.

Pike, K. L. (1967). *Language in relation to a unified theory of the structure of human behavior.* Mouton.

Pirt, G. (1990). Discourse intonation problems for nonnative speakers. In M. Hewings (Ed.), *Papers in discourse intonation* (pp 145–155). University of Birmingham.

Prator, C., & Robinett, B. W. (1985). *Manual of American English pronunciation*. Holt, Rinehart & Winston.

Rampton, B. (1995). *Crossing: Language and ethnicity among adolescents*. Longman.

Rampton, B. (2013). Styling in a language learned later in life. *The Modern Language Journal, 97*(2), 360–382. https://doi.org/10.1111/j.1540-4781.2013.12010.x

Reed, M., & Michaud, C. (2015). Intonation in research and practice: The importance of metacognition. In M. Reed & J. M. Levis (Eds.), *The handbook of English pronunciation* (pp. 454–470). Wiley-Blackwell.

Sapon, S., & Carroll, J. (1958). Discriminative perception of speech sounds as a function of native language. *General Linguistics, 3*(2), 62–72.

Schmidt, M. (1980). Coordinate structures and language universals in interlanguage. *Language Learning, 30*(2), 397–416. https://doi.org/10.1111/j.1467-1770.1980.tb00325.x

Schmidt, R. W. (1987). Sociolinguistic variation and language transfer in phonology. In G. Ioup & S. H. Weinberger (Eds.), *Interlanguage phonology: The acquisition of a second language sound system* (pp. 365–377). Newbury House.

Scholes, R. J. (1968). Phonemic interference as a perceptual problem. *Language and Speech, 11*(2), 86–103. https://doi.org/10.1177%2F002383096801100202

Schumann, J. (1978). *The pidginization process: A model for second language acquisition*. Newbury House.

Scovel, T. (1969). Foreign accents, language acquisition, and cerebral dominance. *Language Learning, 19*(3–4), 245–253. https://doi.org/10.1111/j.1467-1770.1969.tb00466.x

Scovel, T. (1988). *A time to speak: A psycholinguistic inquiry into the critical period for human speech*. Wadsworth.

Selinker, L. (1972). Interlanguage. *International Review of Applied Linguistics in Language Teaching, 10*, 209–231. https://doi.org/10.1515/iral.1972.10.1-4.209

Selinker, L., & Douglas, D. (1985). Wrestling with 'context' in interlanguage theory. *Applied Linguistics, 6*(2), 190–204. https://doi.org/10.1093/applin/6.2.190

Sheldon, A., & Strange, W. (1982). The acquisition of /r/ and /l/ by Japanese learners of English: Evidence that speech production can precede speech perception. *Applied Psycholinguistics, 3*(3), 243–261. https://doi.org/10.1017/S0142716400001417

Singh, S., & Black, J. (1966). Study of twenty-six intervocalic consonants as spoken and recognized by four language groups. *The Journal of the Acoustical Society of America, 39*(2), 372–387. https://doi.org/10.1121/1.1909899

Skinner, B. F. (1957). *Verbal behavior*. Appleton-Century-Crofts.

Smith, J., Meyers, C. M., & Burkhalter, A. (1992). *Communicate: Strategies for international teaching assistants*. Prentice Hall Regents.

Stern, S. (1980). Drama in second language learning from a psycholinguistic perspective. *Language Learning, 30*(1), 77–100. https://doi.org/10.1111/j.1467-1770.1980.tb00152.x

Stevens, K. N., Libermann, A. M., Studdert-Kennedy, M., & Öhman, S. E. G. (1969). Cross-language study of vowel perception. *Language and Speech, 12*(1), 1–23. https://doi.org/10.1177%2F002383096901200101

Stevens, S. G. (1989). A "dramatic" approach to improving the intelligibility of ITAs. *English for Specific Purposes, 8*(2), 181–194. https://doi.org/10.1016/0889-4906(89)90029-X

Stinson, M., & Freebody, K. (2006). The DOL project: The contributions of process drama to improved results in English oral communication. *Youth Theatre Journal, 20*(1), 27–41. https://doi.org/10.1080/08929092.2006.10012585

Tannen, D. (1989). *Talking voices: Repetition, dialogue, and imagery in conversational discourse.* Cambridge University Press.

Tarone, E. (1978). The phonology of interlanguage. In J. C. Richards (Ed.), *Understanding second and foreign language learning* (pp. 15–33). Newbury House.

Tarone, E. (1979). Interlanguage as chameleon. *Language Learning, 29*(1), 181–191. https://doi.org/10.1111/j.1467-1770.1979.tb01058.x

Tarone, E. (1980). Some influences on the syllable structure of interlanguage phonology. *International Review of Applied Linguistics in Language Teaching, 18*(2), 139–152. https://doi.org/10.1515/iral.1980.18.1-4.139

Tarone, E. (1983). On the variability of interlanguage systems. *Applied Linguistics, 4*(2), 142–163. https://doi.org/10.1093/applin/4.2.142

Tarone, E. (1985). Variability in interlanguage use: A study of style-shifting in morphology and syntax. *Language Learning, 35*(3), 373–403. https://doi.org/10.1111/j.1467-1770.1985.tb01083.x

Tarone, E. (1988). *Variation in Interlanguage.* Edward Arnold.

Tarone, E. (1990). On variation in interlanguage: A response to Gregg. *Applied Linguistics, 11*(4), 392–400. https://doi.org/10.1093/applin/11.4.392

Tarone, E. (2000). Still wrestling with 'context' in interlanguage theory. *Annual Review of Applied Linguistics, 20*, 182–198. https://doi.org/10.1017/S0267190500200111

Tarone, E. (2019). Voices in learner language: Language play and double voicing in second language acquisition and use. In M. Haneda & H. Nassaji (Eds.), *Perspectives on language as action: Essays in honour of Merrill Swain* (pp. 177–193). Multilingual Matters.

Tarone, E. (2021). Alphabetic print literacy level and noticing oral corrective feedback in SLA. In H. Nassaji & E. Khartchava (Eds.), *The Cambridge handbook of corrective feedback in second language learning and teaching* (pp. 450–470). Cambridge University Press.

Tarone, E., Bigelow, M., & Hansen, K. (2009). *Literacy and second language oracy.* Oxford University Press.

Tarone, E., & Liu, G.-Q. (1995). Situational context, variation, and second language acquisition theory. In G. Cook & B. Seidlhofer (Eds.), *Principle and practice in applied linguistics: Studies in honour of H. G. Widdowson* (pp. 107–124). Oxford University Press.

Tarone, E., LaScotte, D., Meyers, C., & Moreno, L. (2018). *Voices in learner language: Heteroglossia and language play in SLA* [Panel presentation]. TESOL 2018 International Convention & English Language Expo, Chicago, IL.

Tarone, E., & Meyers, C. (2018). The Mirroring Project: Improving suprasegmentals and intelligibility in ESL presentations. In R. Alonso (Ed.), *Speaking in a second language* (pp. 197–223). John Benjamins.

Taylor, L. L., Guiora, A. Z., Catford, J. C., & Lane, H. L. (1969). The role of personality variables in second language behavior. *Comprehensive Psychiatry, 10*(6), 463–474. https://doi.org/10.1016/0010-440X(69)90082-0

Vang, C. (2013). *'Double-voicing' in constructed dialogue: Investigation of the function of Japanese in bilingual second generation Japanese American dialogue* [Unpublished M.A. qualifying paper]. University of Minnesota, United States. Accessed 21 August 2021 at University of Minnesota Digital Conservancy, http://hdl.handle.net/11299/164768

Vygotsky, L. (1978). *Mind in society: The development of higher psychological processes.* Harvard University Press.

Vygotsky, L. (1981). The genesis of higher mental functions. In J. Wertsch (Ed.), *The concept of activity in Soviet psychology* (pp. 144–188). M. E. Sharpe.

Wennerstrom, A. (1994). Intonational meaning in English discourse: A study of non-native speakers. *Applied Linguistics, 15*(4), 399–420. https://doi.org/10.1093/applin/15.4.399

Wennerstrom, A. (2001). *The music of everyday speech: Prosody and discourse analysis.* Oxford University Press.

Wertsch, J. (1991). *Voices of the mind: A sociocultural approach to mediated action.* Harvard University Press.

Wertsch, J. (2002). *Voices of collective remembering.* Cambridge University Press.

Wode, H. (1976). Developmental sequences in naturalistic second language acquisition. *Working Papers in Bilingualism, 11,* 1–31. Ontario Institute for Studies in Education.

Wode, H. (1977). The L2 acquisition of /r/. *Phonetica, 34*(3), 200–217. https://doi.org/10.1159/000259877

Wode, H. (1980). Phonology in L2 acquisition. In S. Felix (Ed.), *Second language development: Trends and issues* (pp. 123–136). Gunter Narr.

Wong, R. (1987). *Teaching pronunciation: Focus on rhythm.* Center for Applied Linguistics.

Wortham, S. (2001). *Narratives in action: A strategy for research and analysis.* Teachers College Press.

Yates, L. (2017). Learning how to speak: Pronunciation, pragmatics and practicalities in the classroom and beyond. *Language Teaching, 50*(2), 227–246. https://doi.org/10.1017/S0261444814000238

Yates, L. (2021). *Getting the balance right: Language learning in and for the contemporary workplace* [Plenary address]. Annual Conference of the American Association for Applied Linguistics [online (virtual)].

Yuan, J., & Liberman, M. (2014). F0 declination in English and Mandarin broadcast news speech. *Speech Communication, 65*, 67–74. https://doi.org/10.1016/j.specom.2014.06.001

Yule, G. (1993). Reported discourse in contemporary English. *Revista Canaria de Estudios Ingleses, 26-27*, 17–26.

Zielinski, B. W. (2008). The listener: No longer the silent partner in reduced intelligibility. *System, 36*(1), 69–84. https://doi.org/10.1016/j.system.2007.11.004

Zielinski, B. W. (2015). The segmental/suprasegmental debate. In M. Reed & J. M. Levis (Eds.), *The handbook of English pronunciation* (pp. 397–412). Wiley-Blackwell.

Appendix A

Student Worksheets and Handouts for Mirroring Activities in L2 Classrooms

Mirroring a Native or Intelligible Non-Native English Speaker: Student Worksheet 1

<u>What:</u>
Choose a native speaker of English or intelligible non-native speaker that you would like to mirror.

<u>Why:</u>
This project will help you improve your pronunciation in the following ways:
- You will practice body language, or non-verbal cues in effective, comprehensible American English speech.
- You will demonstrate your understanding of the principles of the English sound system by analyzing and reproducing real speech.
- You will demonstrate an understanding of how social role and identity interact with pronunciation by taking on a "role" or "being" someone else.

<u>How:</u>
1. **Choose** someone whose spoken English you admire and would like to sound like. You might choose a TV personality (e.g., newscaster, character on a TV show, movie star), a TED Talk, or a famous political personality (e.g., John F. Kennedy or Michelle Obama). Obtain a video recording of this person speaking. It can be a speech, an advertisement, an interview, a news report, a situation comedy, a movie, or a documentary.

2. You will choose **7–10 consecutive sentences** from the person's speech and **"mirror"** it as closely as you can. You will pretend to "be" them; imitate their body language (gestures, facial expressions, etc.)! In addition, **transcribe** the speech exactly by writing in pauses, stress, and intonation marks.

3. Write the name of the speaker, the title of the video, and the URL below:

   Speaker:

   Title of video:

   URL:

<u>Worksheet:</u>
Please fill out this worksheet.

1. Who are you going to "mirror" for your project? What "role" does this person play in the video recording, e.g., teacher, speaker, news reporter, etc.?

2. Why did you choose this person and this particular scene? (Hint: Think about what makes this person/scene a good choice to imitate. What do you like about this person/scene? On the other hand, what difficulties might you face either with the character or the scene? If it seems too difficult, you may want to choose another person and/or scene.)

3. In the space below (or on the back of this sheet), transcribe the consecutive sentences you will use for your project. Double space because you will need room to mark your transcription for various aspects of pronunciation.

Mirroring Project Analysis & Mark-Up: Student Worksheet 2

Step 1: Overall Impression

With the **sound off**, answer the following questions:
- How do you think the speaker is feeling?
- What do you notice about the way they speak? Do they enunciate (move lips and jaw a lot)? If so, can you identify any of their words (without sound)?

Step 2: Purpose and Tone
- Who's the speaker? What do you know about them?
- What are they trying to do? (educate, persuade, joke, etc.)
- How do they feel about what they're saying?
- Who is their audience?

Step 3: Speech and Non-Verbals
With the **sound on**, answer the following questions:
- How does the speaker make their message effective?
- What about their volume? Is it loud or soft?
- What about their rate of speech? Is it fast or slow?
- How would you characterize their enunciation (a lot or only a little lip and jaw movement)?
- How would you characterize their intonation (up and down of their speech)? Does their intonation vary a lot or only a little?
- Does their speech change at any time during the video? If so, how does it change? Why? For example, sometimes people get louder when they become angry.

Step 4: Mark Transcript
Listen for when the speaker pauses. Draw in a slash mark (/) to indicate a pause and two slash marks to indicate a longer pause (//). This will help you practice and memorize the segment. Then write the word that gets emphasis in capitalized bold letters. Draw an arrow to show how the pitch changes on the emphasized word. Finally, write any body language which the speaker uses above the word or words in which they use it:

(moves head)
So what do we do ↗↘NOW? //

Transcription Practice Activity: Student Worksheet 3

Instructions:
1. Take a script or transcript and turn it into a "poem" with one thought group per line.
2. Write the emphasized word in each thought group or sentence in **BOLD CAPITAL LETTERS.**
3. Read each phrase first, then look up and say it to your instructor or a partner. Take a rubber band and pull it longer as you say the lengthened vowel on the stressed syllable of the emphasized word. This will help you give that vowel length and pitch.

Sample Transcript (from TED Talk)

It also worked the same in her ↗↘**RESEARCH.** //

When she asks people about ↗↘**LOVE,**

they tell her about ↗↘**HEARTBREAK.** //

When she asks people about ↗↘**BELONGING,**

they tell her their most excruciating experiences of being ↗↘**EXCLUDED.** //

And when she asks people about ↗↘**CONNECTION,**

they tell her stories about ↗↘**DISconnection.**//

She didn't ↗↘**UNDERSTAND** it.//

Trial Version Self-Critique: Student Worksheet 4

Instructions:
You have just completed the Trial Version of your Mirroring Project. In preparation for the Final Version, please complete the question below:

Strengths:
- What areas of pronunciation (pausing, prominence, intonation) or non-verbal communication are you doing well?

- Do you think you show the same emotion and tone as the original speaker? Include specific examples below:

Areas for Improvement:
- What, if anything, do you need to change for the Final Version of the Mirroring Project?

- How will you do so?

Final Version Self-Critique: Student Worksheet 5

You have just completed the Final Version of your Mirroring Project. Congratulations!

<u>Please complete the questions below:</u>

Areas of Improvement:
- What improvement do you see between the Trial Version and the Final Version of your Mirroring Project? Write specific examples here:

Continued Improvement:
- What strategies have you developed as a result of this project?

- How will you use these strategies to continue working on your pronunciation, body language, and public speaking skills? Be specific.

Channeling a Model: Student Worksheet 6

Task:
You have just finished your Mirroring Project. Now, as a way to apply what you have learned, you will give a short presentation in which you try to "channel" the person whom you mirrored. In other words, you will try to use your own words and ideas but say the words the way you feel that person would say them – the pausing, the use of body language, the rhythm, stress, and intonation patterns. Your goal is to end up "being" your model speaker.

Step 1: Topic
Write down a 30-second to one-minute speech or make notes for a one-minute presentation. Choose a topic which you are passionate about, e.g., education, the environment, respect for others, etc. Write your speech or notes below.

Step 2: Write
Go back and write in slash marks for pausing, underline words which you want to stress or emphasize and perhaps write down body language which you think will help you convey your ideas in the way your model speaker did. Be conscious of what you have chosen and how you will apply it.

Step 3: Practice
Now, practice your speech or presentation by recording yourself using your cell phone or another recording device. As you give your speech, try to imagine you are "being" your model speaker.

Step 4: Analyze
View your presentation. Do you see yourself applying some of the speech patterns and techniques your model used in his/her presentation? If so, which ones? If not, practice again.

Evaluation of Channeling Project: Student Worksheet 7

<u>As you view your video, answer the questions below:</u>
1. **Overall.** In what ways is your "performance" similar to your original speaker? Comment on any of the areas here: body language, pausing, stress patterns, intonation, enunciation, emotion, etc.

2. Are there any **key words** which you mispronounced or stressed incorrectly? Write them below:
   Example: po-LI-tics should be PO-li-tics

3. Are there any **word endings** which you omitted? Write examples below:
   Example: "Yesterday I stop at your house" should be "Yesterday I stop**ped** at your house."

4. Are there any areas from question number 1 above that you think you still **need to improve** (for example: body language, pausing, stress patterns, intonation, enunciation, emotion)? If so, write them here:

5. What have you **learned** from doing this project? How will you **apply** what you have learned to your future speaking English?

Appendix B

Teacher Notes for the Mirroring Project

This appendix will ideally be used by instructors to help them guide their students through the steps of the Mirroring Project, including how to adapt the Mirroring Project to an online environment for instructors who may be teaching remotely. Examples from classes in which we have used this approach are included to demonstrate specifics. Instructors whose students are at beginning stages of emergent literacy will need to rely heavily on this appendix, since their students will be unable to benefit from the handouts provided in Appendix A.

The Mirroring Project comprises 10 steps, which can be undertaken over a period of three weeks during a semester or term. The steps are:

TABLE B.1. The Mirroring Project in 10 Steps

Analysis Phase	
Step 1	In conjunction with the instructor, students identify their pronunciation and non-verbal challenges.
Step 2	Students choose a model speaker they identify with and select a short (1–2 minute long) video-recorded speech sample.
Step 3	Students analyze their model's speech sample and non-verbals for communicative effectiveness (i.e., speaker's intent and goal) using guiding questions provided by the instructor.
Step 4	Students transcribe their speech sample, identifying and marking for thought groups, prominence, and intonation and adding annotations for non-verbal communication.
Mirroring Phase	
Step 5	Students mirror their model one thought group at a time as they follow their original video recording.
Step 6	Students practice internalizing their model's speech patterns and non-verbal communication features using the "Read, Look Up, and Say" technique.
Step 7	Students are video-recorded during a trial version, speaking to an audience of classmates and the instructor.

Step 8	Students critique the trial version with their instructor, then continue to practice improving their speech patterns and non-verbal communication features as many times as they wish.
Step 9	Students are video-recorded a final time, in front of an audience of classmates and their instructor and analyze and critique the final version.
Channeling Phase	
Step 10	Students write material for the "channeling" stage of the project, where they practice emulating the speech and non-verbal features and style of the model speaker they mirrored, but now delivering ORIGINAL content. Then, students and their instructor evaluate that channeling performance.

The following section explains each step of the Mirroring Project in detail, providing hints and guidelines for helping ensure a successful project.

Analysis Phase

Step 1: Pronunciation and Body Language Challenges

Students undertake some type of diagnostic, such as giving a brief self-introduction, giving a short speech about a topic of interest, and/or engaging in a diagnostic interview. The diagnostic is recorded and then analyzed by the instructor and the student. Areas of interest might include: use of pausing, rate of speech, pitch range, or gestures. Each student, in conjunction with the instructor, comes up with a plan for pronunciation improvement based on the diagnostic analysis.

Step 2: Selection of Model Speaker and Speech Sample

In light of the results of the diagnostic in Step 1, students choose a model speaker (native-English speaker or highly intelligible, comprehensible non-native speaker, cf. Murphy, 2014) based not only on the speaker's suprasegmentals and non-verbal characteristics in a chosen segment, but also based on the student's identification with the model speaker as someone whom they would like to imitate. A list of possible model speakers and segments as well as characteristics of ineffective models (too fast, little pausing, monotonic speech, etc.) may be provided to the class.

A worksheet (Appendix A, Worksheet 1) is provided to guide students in identifying possible models and segments for their project. A crucial step in the process is to allow the instructor access to the worksheet to vet the choice of speaker and segment before even beginning to have the students undertake the project. Valuable time can be wasted trying to convince students that their model is inappropriate and searching for a substitute. Sometimes, instructors may be aware of segments or speakers that they think would be a good "fit" for a particular student and can guide them appropriately to consider such segments.

Step 3: Segment Purpose and Tone

An important part of the mirroring process is to focus on what the purpose and tone of the segment are. For this reason, students identify the underlying purpose (persuasion, providing information, and/or entertainment), speech characteristics (e.g., volume, rate of speech, pausing, intonation) and ways in which non-verbal communication (e.g., use of space, gestures, facial expressions) contribute to the pronunciation features and underlying purpose. For instance, gestures often are synchronized with stress patterns (Hardison, 2016), and eyebrow movements often correspond to changes in pitch (Hardison, 2016). They also pay attention to whether any of these areas change during the segment and try to understand why. For example, a model speaker may speak loudly with less pitch variation when they show anger. See Appendix A, Worksheet 2.

Step 4: Speech/Non-verbal Analysis

During this step, students either transcribe the segment themselves or download it from the Internet. Next, they analyze the speech for the features of pronunciation they are working on. For instance, a student who tends to speak without pausing or in a monotone voice will mark their segment for pausing and prominence. Due to the fact that non-verbal communication often coincides with or highlights verbal messages, they will note the model speaker's facial expressions and gestures and annotate them next to the word or phrase accompanying that movement. Once completed, students will share their marked transcription with their instructor to check for accuracy. A sample marked transcription is included below:

Michelle Obama: 9:13 – 9:50
https://www.youtube.com/watch?v=CX9CONduxJs

Instructions: As you listen to the next speech "paragraph" by Michelle Obama, do the following:
1. Mark the pauses AND thought groups with a rightward slash: /.
2. Write the word that gets emphasis in **CAPITALIZED BOLD LETTERS.** If the word has more than one syllable, underline the stressed syllable.
3. Draw in arrows to indicate intonation.
4. Write in body language in parentheses ( ) next to the words where non-verbals appear.

But let's be ➔**CLEAR** (*eyes*) / going high does ↗↘**NOT** (*raises eyebrows*) mean / putting on a ↗**SMILE** and saying nice ↗↘**THINGS** (*shakes head*) / when ↗↘**CONFRONTED** (*nod*) by ↗**VICIOUSNESS** (*moves head*) and ↗↘**CRUELTY.** (*moves head*) / Going ↗↘**HIGH** means taking (*uses right hand*) / the ↗↘**HARDER** (*uses right hand*) path. / It means / ↗**SCRAPING** and ↗↘**CLAWING** (*uses both hands*) our way to that ↗↘**MOUNTAIN TOP.** (*raises one hand*) / Going ↗↘**HIGH** means / (*raises her head*) **STANDING** ↗↘**FIERCE AGAINST** ↗↘**HATRED** (*slow and raises right hand*) / while ↗↘**REMEMBERING** (*nods head*) that ➔**WE** are (*two fists*) ↗↘**ONE NATION** under **GOD** (*nods her head*) / and if we want to ↗**SURVIVE** (*points finger*) / (*soft*) we've **GOT** to **FIND** a **WAY** to live ➔**TOGETHER** (*raises her hand and shakes head*) / and ↗↘**WORK** (*uses hands*) together ➔**ACROSS** (*moves hand*) our ↗↘**DIFFERENCES.** (*moves head*)

Mirroring Phase

Step 5: Mirror Model

Now that students have zoomed in to the segment and analyzed it, they zoom out again and focus on putting each thought group into their short-term memory. They access the original video and click "pause" after each thought group or sentence. They then say that phrase or sentence immediately afterward, focusing on mirroring the exact words and imitating the body language of the original speaker. If necessary, they can first mirror the spoken language and then add the body language. They should make eye contact with the original speaker and say each phrase looking at the original speaker. So, using the previous transcript as an example, the student would mirror the first thought group, "But let's be **CLEAR** (*eyes*)" making sure the word "clear" is emphasized and using their eyes to highlight the word, followed by a short pause. They would then go on to the next phrase, "going high does **NOT** (*raises eyebrows*) mean" by again focusing on spoken language and body language. The process would repeat itself until the end of the segment.

Step 6: Internalizing Speech (Practice Activity)

Up to this point, students have familiarized themselves with the original speaker, but it is now time to internalize the speech so as to make it their own. They do this by using their marked transcript and reading each thought group, looking up, and saying it to partner. The audience may consist of one other person or a group of listeners, but the key is that there is a real person for this step.

Appendix A, Worksheet 3 illustrates how students should undertake this activity. It includes a sample marked transcript. Notice how each thought group takes up one line. This is deliberate so that students consciously learn to pause between thought groups and not to think about more than one thought group at a time. If students are having a hard time making emphasized words long enough or changing pitch, they can practice using a rubber band and/or hand movements for pitch movement.

Notes for Instructors:
1. Students shouldn't read out loud from the paper. They should use the Read, Look Up, and Say technique.
2. Students should only use a rubber band for emphasized words.
3. Pitch should go up and then come down on the STRESSED syllable of the emphasized word, e.g., be↗LONG↘ing.

Step 7: Trial Version

Students are now ready to perform the "Trial Version" of the Mirroring Project. If students are in a class or a lab, each person can come up to the front and perform the same way as they have done in Step 6, except this time they are performing for the audience, which is made up of the other class members, as well as the instructor. Students are video-recorded, after which their audience members give them feedback on how well they have done. This feedback from others is crucial as it can provide valuable feedback for the speaker so that they can know where to focus for the final version. In addition, by providing feedback, audience members are developing critical thinking skills to help them determine what makes an effective communicator.

Step 8: Trial Version Critique

After class, students view their "trial" version and complete a self-critique in which they identify strengths and challenges of that performance. Employing a top-down perspective, they analyze suprasegmentals (pausing, prominence, and intonation) as well as how effectively they are capturing the emotions and tone of the original speaker. See Appendix A, Worksheet 4.

At this point, the instructor may also view the trial version of the video and provide feedback on strengths and perhaps one challenge that they feel would make the biggest difference in the final version. Of course, specific examples and/or suggestions for change should be included. If the instructor has access to audio or video, suggestions can be recorded.

Step 9: Final Version and Analysis

The big day is here! For the final version of this project, each student again performs the segment; however, this time they are expected to have memorized it so that they do not need the transcript. If desired, they can bring props or dress as the original speaker. The main focus this time should be expressing the emotion and intent of the model speaker. Should they make a mistake or forget a word or even a phrase, they should be encouraged to ad lib. They can also record more than once if they are dissatisfied with their first attempt.

Again, students will complete a self-critique; however, the focus this time is on what they have improved from their trial version. They should also reflect on what strategies they have developed which can help them continue improving beyond the scope of the current project. See Appendix A, Worksheet 5.

Channeling Phase

Step 10: Channeling and Evaluation

Clearly, it is not enough to simply mirror a model speaker to ensure transfer to a speaker's own speech patterns; the *Channeling Phase* was added to the Mirroring Project as a way to affect such transfer. Channeling involves asking students to perform (in front of an audience) content that is their own, such as a previously recorded talk, a self-introduction, a written speech, etc., while trying to channel the voice of their model speaker – communicating their own material the way they think their model would have said it using verbal and non-verbal aspects of their model's speech. Appendix A, Worksheet 6 explains this part of the project in detail to students, and Appendix A, Worksheet 7 helps students to analyze their performance in the channeling portion of the project.

Adaptation to an Online Environment

The Mirroring Project and Channeling can be done either in a face-to-face or in an online environment, such as Zoom or Google Hangouts. If undertaken in an online environment, several adjustments can be made. For instance, students can be put into breakout rooms as they practice Step 6: Internalizing Speech Segment. If there's not time for all students to perform their trial or final versions during class, they can use an alternate platform, such as Flip (2022; formerly Flipgrid), to make a recording and share it with the rest of the class. Alternatively, if the class consists of too many students to share with everyone, the instructor can assign members to smaller groups and ask those students to serve as audience members for each other.

Before beginning either the Mirroring Project or the Channeling piece, it is a good idea to share an example with the class so that students have a clear idea of what the goal of the project is. Instructors can even share an example of a Trial Version so that students can easily see that there is not any pressure to do a "perfect" job the first time. As they view examples, they can undertake some general critiques to begin the process of analyzing effective communication, thereby internalizing these characteristics into their own communication.

Author Index

Printed in the USA
CPSIA information can be obtained
at www.ICGtesting.com
JSHW070110141223
53785JS00009B/57